# Global Entrepreneurship Monitor India Report 2021/22

## A National Study on Entrepreneurship

# Global Entrepreneurship Monitor India Report 2021/22

## A National Study on Entrepreneurship

*Authored by*

**Sunil Shukla**
*Director-General Entrepreneurship Development Institute of India*

**Pankaj Bharti**
*Associate Professor, Entrepreneurship Development Institute of India*

**Amit Kumar Dwivedi**
*Associate Professor, Entrepreneurship Development Institute of India*

Routledge
Taylor & Francis Group

First published 2024
by Routledge
4 Park Square, Milton Park, Abingdon, Oxon OX14 4RN

and by Routledge
605 Third Avenue, New York, NY 10158

*Routledge is an imprint of the Taylor & Francis Group, an informa business*

© 2024 Sunil Shukla et. al.

*British Library Cataloguing-in-Publication Data*
A catalogue record for this book is available from the British Library

ISBN: 978-1-032-48428-0 (pbk)

Typeset in Century Schoolbook
by Aditiinfosystems

# Table of Contents

*List of Figures* — *vii*

*List of Tables* — *ix*

*Author's Profile* — *xi*

*Acknowledgements* — *xiii*

*Executive Summary* — *xv*

1. **Business and Entrepreneurship Perspectives in India During Post-Covid-19: A Period of Economic Recovery** — 1

2. **Global Entrepreneurship Monitor (GEM) Conceptual Framework** — 10

3. **Measuring Entrepreneurship Activity in India** — 19

4. **Entrepreneurial Framework Conditions in India: National Expert Survey (NES)** — 39

5. **Entrepreneurial Activities and Entrepreneurship Ecosystems In India** — 59

*About Entrepreneurship Development Institute of India, Ahmedabad* — *67*

*Appendix* — *70*

*Bibliography* — *102*

# List of Figures

| | | |
|---|---|---|
| 1.1 | Global Economic Outlook for Select Indicators | 2 |
| 1.2 | Global Trade Resilience During the COVID-19 Pandemic Than During the 2008–09 Global Financial Crisis | 3 |
| 1.3 | Growth Rate of Select Macroeconomic Indicators of Indian Economy (Constant Prices Base Year: 2011–12) | 4 |
| 1.4 | India's External Sector Performance | 5 |
| 1.5 | Unemployment Rate By Age Group 15 Years and Above in India, Urban Persons | 6 |
| 1.6 | Start-up Ecosystem in India (2015–22) | 7 |
| 1.7 | Major Sector of Start-ups that Emerged During COVID-19 | 7 |
| 1.8 | Funding Deals and Amount for EdTech Start-ups in India | 8 |
| 1.9 | Funding Trend in Health Tech in India | 8 |
| 2.1 | The GEM Conceptual Framework | 13 |
| 2.2 | Entrepreneurship Phases and GEM Entrepreneurship Indicators | 14 |
| 3.1 | Attitudes and Perception of Males and Females in India | 23 |
| 3.3 | Attitudes and Perception: A Comparison in Low-Income Countries | 24 |
| 3.2 | Attitudes and Perception: A Comparison of BRICS Countries | 24 |
| 3.4 | Perception and Attitudes: A Comparison of the Indian Region | 25 |
| 3.5 | Attitude and Perception: Urban–Rural Comparison | 26 |
| 3.6 | TEA, EBA, and EEA in India | 26 |
| 3.7 | Region-wise Total Entrepreneurship Activities | 27 |
| 3.8 | Total Early-Stage Entrepreneurial Activity: Region-Wise and Gender-Wise | 28 |
| 3.9 | TEA of Low-Income Countries and Gender-Wise Comparison | 28 |
| 3.10 | TEA of BRICS Countries | 29 |
| 3.11 | Age Group and Education-Wise TEA in India | 29 |
| 3.12 | TEA of Low-Income Countries with Age-Group Comparison | 30 |
| 3.13 | Education Level-Wise TEA in Low-Income Countries | 31 |
| 3.14 | Business Exit and TEA: A Comparison of Low-Income Countries | 31 |
| 3.15 | Reasons for Business Exit: A Comparison of Low-Income Countries | 32 |
| 3.16 | Entrepreneurial Motivation: A Comparison of Low-Income Countries in GEM | 33 |

| | | |
|---|---|---:|
| 3.17 | Growth Expectation of Job Creation in Low-Income Countries in GEM | 34 |
| 3.18 | Sectors for Starting a Business | 35 |
| 3.19 | Pandemic as Opportunities for New Business | 36 |
| 3.20 | Pandemic as Problems for New Business | 37 |
| 3.21 | Use of Digital Technology for Business | 37 |
| 4.1 | Entrepreneurial Framework Conditions | 40 |
| 4.2 | Entrepreneurial Framework Conditions of India and Comparison with Low-Income and GEM Countries | 41 |
| 4.3 | Entrepreneurial Framework Conditions of Low-Income Countries | 42 |
| 4.4 | Financial Environment Related to Entrepreneurship in India | 43 |
| 4.5 | Easiness to Get Financing for Entrepreneurs in India | 44 |
| 4.6 | Government Support and Policies in India | 45 |
| 4.7 | Taxes and Bureaucracy in India | 45 |
| 4.8 | Government Programs in India | 46 |
| 4.9 | Education (Primary and Secondary) in India | 47 |
| 4.10 | Education (Post-secondary level) in India | 47 |
| 4.11 | Research and Development in India | 48 |
| 4.12 | Professional and Commercial Infrastructure Access in India | 49 |
| 4.13 | Internal Market Dynamics in India | 49 |
| 4.14 | Internal Market Burden in India | 50 |
| 4.15 | Physical Infrastructure in India | 51 |
| 4.16 | Social and Cultural Norms in India | 52 |
| 4.17 | Support to Digitalization and Telework | 53 |
| 4.18 | Gig Economy and Gig-Based Business Model | 53 |
| 4.19 | Environment Protection and Awareness | 54 |
| 4.20 | Government Decisions and Measures to Control the Effect of Pandemic | 54 |
| 4.21 | Support to Women Entrepreneurship and Conciliation | 55 |
| 4.22 | Positive Impact on Entrepreneurship Ecosystem | 56 |
| 4.23 | Negative Impact on Entrepreneurship Ecosystem | 56 |
| 4.24 | Fostering Factors for Entrepreneurial Activity in India | 57 |
| 4.24 | Recommendations to Improve Entrepreneurial Activity in India | 58 |
| 5.1 | Trends of Individual Attributes in India | 60 |
| 5.2 | Total Entrepreneurship Activities in India in Last 5 Years | 61 |
| 5.3 | Entrepreneurial Finance and Government Policy for Entrepreneurship | 62 |
| 5.4 | Market Dynamics, R&D and Infrastructure in the Last 5 Years | 63 |
| 5.5 | Education and Culture & Social Norms for Entrepreneurship in India | 63 |
| 5.6 | Fostering Factors for Entrepreneurship | 65 |
| 5.7 | Recommendation for Promoting Entrepreneurship in India | 66 |

# List of Tables

| 1.1 | Growth Rate of Select Macroeconomic Indicators of Indian Economy (Constant Prices Base Year: 2011–12) (%) | 4 |
|---|---|---|
| 1.2 | India's External Sector Performance (US$ billion) | 5 |
| 1.3 | Unemployment Rate in India | 5 |
| 2.1 | Economies in GEM 2021, Classified by Income ($GDP per Capita) | 12 |
| 2.2 | Regional Distribution of APS | 16 |
| 2.3 | Rural/Urban Distribution | 17 |
| 2.4 | Gender Distribution | 17 |
| 2.5 | Experts' Specialization (includes Multiple Responses) | 17 |
| 2.6 | Experts' Education | 18 |
| 3.1 | GEM India Snapshot | 20 |
| 3.2 | Attitudes and Perception to Start a Business in India | 21 |
| 3.3 | Impact of COVID | 22 |

# Author's Profile

**Sunil Shukla (Ph.D., Psychology)**

Director General
Entrepreneurship Development Institute of India
National Team Leader, GEM India
Email: sunilshukla@ediindia.org

Dr. Sunil Shukla, Director General of Entrepreneurship Development Institute of India, Ahmedabad, has been closely working, for more than three decades now, in entrepreneurship education, research, training and institution building. Dr. Shukla has envisioned and designed innovative, outcome based programmes and developmental interventions in the domains of 'entrepreneurship', 'start ups' and 'intrapreneurship' for varied target groups including potential & existing entrepreneurs, innovators, faculty, business executives, bankers, managers, disadvantaged sections, family business successors, administrators and business counsellors. And entrepreneurship exponent, Dr. Shukla's work has also left an indelible impact on the grounds of Greater Mekong Subregion (GMS) countries, Asia, Africa, America, Iran and Uzbekistan. His research work has led to notable policy advocacy and decisions. He leads the largest and the most prestigious annual study of entrepreneurial dynamics in the world – the *Global Entrepreneurship Monitor (GEM) India Chapter*. Today several organizations and departments are benefitting from his guidance and mentorship by having him on their Boards.

**Pankaj Bharti (Ph.D. Psychology)**

Associate Professor
Entrepreneurship Development Institute of India
National Team Member, GEM India
Email: pbharti@ediindia.org

Dr. Pankaj Bharti specialises in Organisational Behaviour, Human Resource Management and Corporate Entrepreneurship. He is trained in conceptualising and developing measurement tools for social science research. He holds more than 16 years of experience in academics and industry. He is associated with over 20 National as well as international research projects. He is also a National Team Member of Global Entrepreneurship Monitor (GEM), India and he is co-author of GEM India Report 2014, 2015/16, 2016/17, 2017/18, 2018/19 and 2019/20. His core competency lies in psychometric assessment administration and reporting.

**Amit Kumar Dwivedi (Ph.D., Commerce)**

Associate Professor
Entrepreneurship Development Institute of India
National Team Member, GEM India
Email: akdwivedi@ediindia.org

Dr. Amit Kumar Dwivedi has over 17 years of teaching and research experience. He has earned a doctoral degree in Industrial Finance from Lucknow University. His areas of interest are Entrepreneurship Education, Family Business and SME Policy. Dr. Dwivedi has published his research in various leading journals. He is part of the India Team that leads the prestigious 'Global Entrepreneurship Monitor' research study. Also, he is co-author of GEM India Report 2014, 2015/16, 2016/17, 2017/18, 2018/19 and 2019/20. Dr. Dwivedi is trained in Application of Simulation for Entrepreneurship Teaching at the University of Tennessee, USA.

# Acknowledgements

The GEM India Consortium is glad to probe the conditions that enable entrepreneurship to flourish or deteriorate so that suitable interventions could be accordingly instituted. The consortium has been constantly putting in efforts to research the ways and means that could bolster the entrepreneurship scenario so that the entrepreneurs, the lifeblood of economies, continue to perform a potent role.

The GEM Report 2021–2022 throws light on entrepreneurial trends and practices amidst changing business and the impact of COVID-19 on entrepreneurial activities in the country. We express gratitude to the Centre for Research in Entrepreneurship Education and Development (CREED) for providing financial support for this project.

- Our sincere thanks to the GEM Global Team at London Business School, Babson College and the GEM Data Team for their untiring support and direction.

- We would also like to heartily thank the national experts and the respondents of various surveys for sparing their valuable time and sharing rich insights with us.

- We express our gratitude to Dr. Sanjay Kumar Mangla without whose support this task could not have been completed.

- The authors thank Ms. Julie Shah, Head Department of Institutional Communication and Public Relations for facilitating the publication of this report.

- We also thank to Ms. Simran Sodhi, Mr. Ashutosh Mishra and Mr. Kumar Anubhav for their support while the survey and report development.

- We express our cordial thanks to the team members of Kantar, India for timely conducting and submitting data of APS.

Authors

# Executive Summary

The Global Entrepreneurship Monitor (GEM) is a global study conducted by GEM consortium with the aim to collect internationally comparative primary data on entrepreneurial activity and its related concepts. The study has a noble mission to generate global comparative data to understand the entrepreneurial activity. This would help identify factors determining national levels of entrepreneurial activity, as well as policies aimed at enhancing entrepreneurial activity. It measures entrepreneurship through surveys and interviews of field experts conducted by the teams in the respective countries. The GEM survey generates a variety of relevant primary data on different aspects of entrepreneurship and provides harmonized measures about individuals' attributes and their activities in different phases of venturing (from nascent to start-up, established business, and discontinuation).

The present report provides insights into entrepreneurial activities in India. The GEM India study was conducted using a well-established GEM research methodology that is consistent across all participating countries, thus enabling cross-country comparison. The Adult Population Survey (APS) was conducted among 3252 samples and provides information regarding the level of entrepreneurial activity in the country based on the national framework conditions, whereas the National Expert Survey (NES) was conducted on 72 national experts with an average work experience of 10 years. The NES focuses on entrepreneurial start-up eco-system in India with regard to nine entrepreneurial framework conditions (EFCs).

## Key Points from the Adult Population Survey

- The report covers the trend of growth in entrepreneurial activities as well as required individual attributes for starting business. The total entrepreneurship activities rate (TEA) in India has increased from 9.3% in 2017–18 to 14.4% in 2021–22. Along with TEA, nascent entrepreneurship and new business ownership both have increased significantly in same period of time. The increase in nascent entrepreneurship is 4.9% in 2017–18 to 7.2% in 2021–22. Similarly, in the case of New Business Ownership it is from 4.4% to 7.1% for the same period of time. On the similar line, the established entrepreneurship rate has also increased from 6.2% to 8.5% from 2017–18 to 2021–22.

- It is also evident that COVID-19 pandemic has significant affected on the entrepreneurship activities and its related dimensions. The results presented in this report indicate that there is a significant decline in almost all dimensions of entrepreneurship activity in the year of 2020–2021.

- It is evident that there is a significant growth for all five indicators of individual attributes. It implies that youth of the country now perceive that they have better opportunities and they are more capable with well-defined intention to start the business. They are also thinking that starting a new business now is easier than a few years back. It is very clear that the perception of our youth for all attributes is much higher in 2021–22 than 2017–18.

- The finding of this report shows that 83.4% of the population perceives that there is a good opportunity to start a business in their area. Out of the 47 economies who participated, India has ranked second for perceived opportunities.

- About 86% of youth perceived that they have sufficient skills and knowledge to start a business. Out of the 47 economies who participated, India has ranked fourth for perceived capability.

- About 54% of youth have reported that they are not able to start the business due to the fear of failure. The ranking of India is second among GEM participating economies.

- Entrepreneurial intention is a very important part of the research and highlights the possibility of people getting into business. Entrepreneurial intentions are 18.1% for this year and ranking of India is 21st among all the 47 participating economies.

- However, about 82% of youth believe that starting a business is easy in India. The data has greatly improved for easiness to start a business in India. Out of the 47 economies who participated, India has ranked fourth on this parameter. It shows the ease of doing business in India.

- The rate of total early-stage entrepreneurship (TEA) in India has also improved from 5.4% in 2020–21 to 14.4% in 2021–22 and India now ranks 18th among 47 economies surveyed. Total early-stage entrepreneurial activity is indicator of growth of the entrepreneurship development in the country.

- Among female adults, TEA has increased significantly as 12.3% of the total female population are engaged in entrepreneurship in India as compared to 16.3% of the male. The male female difference still exists and needs to be worked on to improve female representation in the overall TEA of the country.

- The findings of this report also reveal that in 2021–22, 8.5% of population is engaged in established business.

- The data of motivation for entrepreneurship is now more refined and very relevant to the entrepreneurship development in the country. About 76% of the people in India want to start a business to make a difference in the world. The percentage is higher for youth in the age group of 18–34 years and it is 78% male in the population. Another important category is to earn living because jobs are scarce and data shows that 91.5% of the population is motivated by this and 91% of youth in the age group of 18–34 years and 92% of youth in the age group of 35–64 years are motivated by the same objective of earn living because jobs are scarce.

- Among the youth of the country, 74% are motivated because they want to continue their family tradition and the same number of youths has reported that they are motivated to earn great wealth.

## Key Takes from NES

- The NES is the second essential survey conducted by GEM every year and this year it was conducted in 50 economies and results are summed up in a newly formed National Entrepreneurship Context Index (NECI). NECI identifies the capacity of the ecosystem of a particular country for the enhancement of entrepreneurship in that country.

- It is evident from the findings that expert's rating has increased in the last 5 years for almost all indicators of EFCs. However, the rating of all EFCs is highest in the financial year 2020–21. It indicates that after lockdown, government has taken extra efforts for developing and strengthen entrepreneurship in the country.

- NES survey in India is based on 72 individual experts from the field of entrepreneurship, start-up, and academics. Experts from various fields directly or indirectly involved with the entrepreneurship domain, suggest new things toward the improvement of the EFCs. About 35% of experts reported that access to physical infrastructure is one of most promising factors for the strengthening of the entrepreneurship ecosystem of the country.

- Experts have also given their suggestions and recommendations for improving overall entrepreneurial ecosystem of the country. The four major points given by experts are to improve financial support, education and training, government programs, and cultural and social norms for entrepreneurship development in the country.

- Out of the low-income economies, India has been tremendously good as an entrepreneurial ecosystem. India is a leading ecosystem for entrepreneurs as compared to the other low-income economies, across all pillars of framework conditions.

- The GEM NECI provides policymakers with insights on how to foster such an environment. The NECI summarizes the assessment of EFCs into a single composite score for the ease of starting and developing a business. The index measures the 12 entrepreneurial environment conditions (EECs) that make up the context in which entrepreneurial activity takes place in a country.

# Business and Entrepreneurship Perspectives in India During Post-Covid-19: A Period of Economic Recovery

1

## 1.1   Introduction

The world is facing the biggest pandemic of all time, COVID-19 which started in Wuhan, China in December 2019. The pandemic has not left any geographical area untouched and caused over six million deaths with over 600 million confirmed cases across the globe. Several countries are still facing continuing waves of COVID-19.

The pandemic hit hard the global economy on almost all economic fronts including economic growth, employment, trade, financing, industrial, agricultural output, etc. This dent in the global economy was multiplied due to the Russia–Ukraine war, which is causing other economic problems like rise in prices of important cereals and petroleum products. This is clearly evident from Figure 1.1 which shows a high dip in all global activity indicators including industrial production, global trade volumes, new manufacturing orders and new services businesses during the pandemic period. Almost all economies globally are experiencing high rates of inflation, and due to Russia–Ukraine war, primarily; international cereal prices have also witnessed a sharp rise.

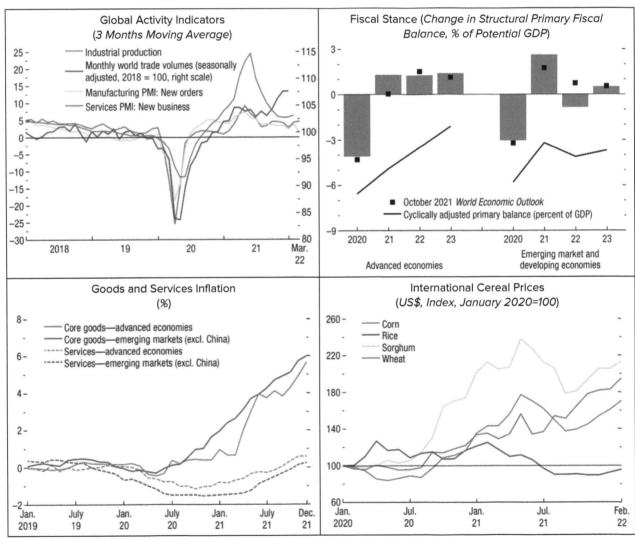

FIGURE 1.1   Global Economic Outlook for Select Indicators

**Source:** *World Economic Outlook, International Monetary Fund, 2022*

The COVID-19 pandemic has put excessive stress on the global trading system and generated unprecedented shocks to the cross-border supply chains. "In 2020, the value of global trade in goods and services in nominal dollar terms fell by 9.6 per cent, while global GDP fell by 3.3 per cent, in the most severe recession since World War II," World Trade Report 2021.[1]

The trade data (Figure 1.2) shows that the global trading system has been more resilient during the COVID-19 crisis as compared to the global financial crisis of 2008–09. This has helped the countries to have access to critical medical supplies, essential food and consumer goods, and also supported them in their economic recovery process.

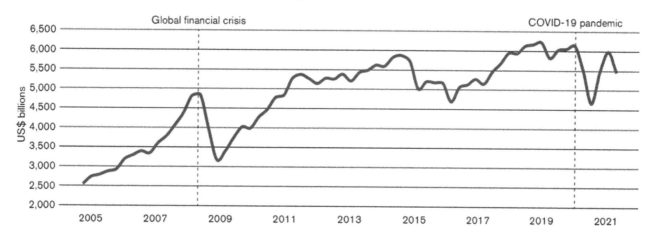

FIGURE 1.2    Global Trade Resilience During the COVID-19 Pandemic Than During the 2008–09 Global Financial Crisis

**Source:** World Trade Report 2021

Today, countries are more hyper-connected and have deeper trade links. This has made them more vulnerable to global shocks as it has been observed during COVID-19. In such a case, it is more important to make global trade more resilient which requires more global cooperation on all fronts including political, economic, cultural, climate, etc.

In this direction, India has played a significant role not only at the domestic level but also at the international level. On one hand, the Indian government helped several countries by providing COVID-19 vaccines and other stuff to fight the pandemic, on the other hand, the country successfully played its role in terms of international cooperation by helping international organizations and other countries to decide upon critical issues of global importance including trade, climate, peace, sectoral cooperation, etc.

India has been in the front runners in fighting COVID-19 despite its big population size (1.40 billion approximately) and was able to develop its own vaccines (Covishield and Covaxin) along with other preventive equipment such as PPE kits, alcohol-based sanitizers, and face masks and treatment medicines for curing this deadly pandemic. According to the Ministry of External Affairs, Government of India, *India has supplied almost 255 million vaccines to over 100 countries/organizations till August 2022.*[2]

Apart from fighting directly on the ground to save people's life and stopping the spread of COVID-19; the Government of India has brought several economic reforms including deregulation of sectors, simplification and digitization of business processes, removal of legacy issues including retrospective tax, privatization, easing norms for inviting foreign investments, and many more. *These reforms have contributed to making India the fifth-largest economy in the world, recently, overtaking Britain.*[3]

---

[1]World Trade Report 2021: Economic resilience and trade (wto.org) Pg. 6
[2]Vaccine Supply (mea.gov.in)
[3]India becomes fifth largest economy in world: A perspective – ThePrint – ANIFeed

## 1.2  Indian Economy During COVID-19 and its Economic Recovery Path

As India is also not an exception, its economy was also severely hit by the pandemic during the financial year 2020–2021, peak pandemic period was marked by country-wide lockdowns and a fall in economic activities. The period caused fatalities with a heavy burden on its health system and an adverse impact on its economy measured in terms of major economic variables including gross domestic product (GDP), exports, industrial growth, employment, etc. However, the country managed the pandemic quite well as it not only could control the spread of the virus but also succeeded in stabilizing the economy.

TABLE 1.1   Growth Rate of Select Macroeconomic Indicators of Indian Economy (Constant Prices Base Year: 2011–12) (%)

| Indicator | 2019–20 | 2020–21 | 2021–22 |
|---|---|---|---|
| Gross Value Added at Basic Prices | 3.81 | −4.80 | 8.11 |
| Gross Domestic Product | 3.74 | −6.60 | 8.68 |
| Per Capita Net National Income | 2.32 | −9.72 | 7.49 |
| Industrial Production (Manufacturing) | −1.40 | −9.60 | 11.80 |
| Industrial Production (General) | −0.80 | −8.40 | 11.40 |
| Agriculture Production (All Crops) | 5.36 | −4.47 | 3.09 |
| Wholesale Price Index (All Commodities) | 1.70 | 1.30 | 13.00 |

**Source:** *Handbook of Statistics on Indian Economy, Reserve Bank of India, 2022*

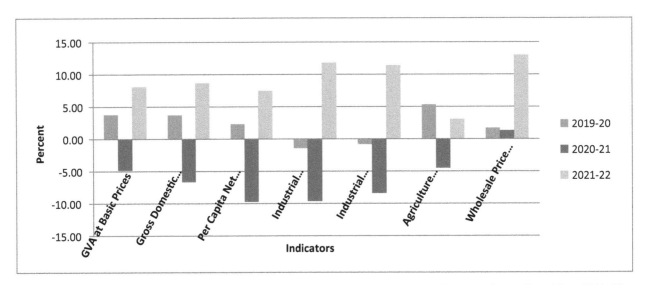

FIGURE 1.3   Growth Rate of Select Macroeconomic Indicators of Indian Economy (Constant Prices Base Year: 2011–12)

The growth rate of major macroeconomic indicators of the Indian economy during pre-COVID (2019–20), during-COVID (2020–21), and during the post-COVID economic recovery period (2021–22) are presented in Table 1.1 and displayed in Figure 1.3. It is clearly evident from the both table and figure that the Indian economy registered a negative growth rate during the COVID-19 period (i.e., 2020–21) for all macroeconomic indicators including gross value added (GVA), GDP, per capita net national income, industrial production, and agriculture production. Whereas, the economy started recovering during 2021–22 and the growth rate of all these indicators turned positive from negative.

Per Capita Net National Income growth rate became 7.49% in 2021–22 from −9.72% in 2020–21 which led to an increase in purchasing power of the people and supported the economy in generating domestic demand, whose positive results were reflected in GDP growth rate (8.68% in 2021–22 from −6.60% in 2020–21). Further, the industrial sector of the economy also started recovering from the pandemic shock when industrial units across the country stopped operations and registered a growth rate of 11.40% in 2021–22 (YoY). The agriculture sector also started its recovery in the last financial year; however, its growth rate is still below the pre-pandemic level. Despite a progressive performance on all these economic fronts, the Indian economy is grappling with a high inflation rate (13% in 2021–22) which is a cause of worry and the government along with the Central Bank of the country is taking measures to control the high rise in prices.

TABLE 1.2    India's External Sector Performance (US$ billion)

| Indicators | 2019–20 | 2020–21 | 2021–22 |
|---|---|---|---|
| Exports | 313.36 | 291.81 | 422.00 |
| Foreign Exchange Reserves | 477.81 | 576.98 | 607.31 |
| Foreign Direct Investment | 56.01 | 54.93 | 56.23 |

*Source: Handbook of Statistics on Indian Economy, Reserve Bank of India, 2022*

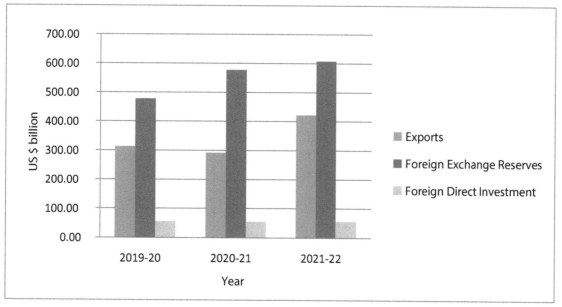

FIGURE 1.4    India's External Sector Performance

The Indian economy has registered economic recovery on external fronts also. The country's exports and foreign direct investment (FDI), which declined during the pandemic, are also on their way to recovery. Exports from India declined to US$ 291.81 billion in 2020–21 from the pre-pandemic level of US$ 313.36 billion in 2019–20 but increased to US$ 422 billion in 2021–22. Similarly, FDI in the country declined to US$ 54.93 billion in 2020–21 from the pre-pandemic level of US$ 56.01 billion in 2019–20, but increased to US$ 56.23 billion in 2021–22. However, the foreign exchange reserves of the country kept on increasing even during the pandemic period. Data on exports, foreign exchange reserves, and FDI are given in Table 1.2 and Figure 1.4.

TABLE 1.3    Unemployment Rate in India

| Year | By Age Group : 15 years and above | | | |
|---|---|---|---|---|
| | Urban-Person | | | |
| | Apr–Jun | Jul–Sep | Oct–Dec | Jan–Mar |
| 2019-20 | 8.9 | 8.3 | 7.8 | 9.1 |
| 2020-21 | 20.8 | 13.2 | 10.3 | 9.3 |
| 2021-22 | 12.6 | 9.8 | 8.7 | 8.2 |

*Source: Periodic Labour Force Survey*

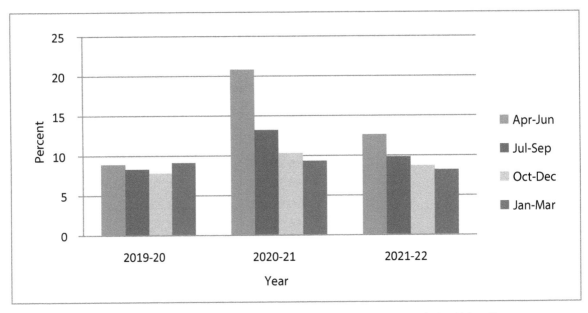

FIGURE 1.5   Unemployment Rate By Age Group 15 Years and Above in India, Urban Persons

Another important factor while discussing economic recovery is the unemployment rate, Table 1.3 and Figure 1.5 reveal that the labour market of the country is also on its way to recovery as the unemployment rate in India is even below its pre-pandemic level (8.2% during Jan–Mar 2021–22 while 9.1% during the same quarter of 2019–20). Figure 1.4 clearly shows that the bars of unemployment rate are quite higher in 2020–21 as compared to the pre-pandemic level which has declined during the period of economic recovery.

### Current State of Indian Economy—Highlights from Economic Survey 2021–22

- Indian economy (GDP) was estimated to grow by 9.2% in real terms in 2021–22 (as per the first advanced estimates of the Economic Survey 2021–22), however, the actual growth rate of the economy in 2021–22 was 8.68%.

- GDP is projected to grow by 8%–8.5% in real terms in 2022–23.

- The year ahead is poised for a pickup in private sector investment with the financial system in a good position to provide support for the economy's revival.

- Projection is comparable with the World Bank and Asian Development Bank's latest forecasts of real GDP growth of 8.7 % and 7.5%, respectively, for 2022–23.

- As per IMF's latest World Economic Outlook projections, India's real GDP is projected to grow at 9% in 2021–22 and 2022–23 and at 7.1% in 2023–2024, which would make India the fastest growing major economy in the world for all the 3 years.

- Macroeconomic stability indicators suggest that the Indian economy is well placed to take on the challenges of 2022–23.

- A combination of high foreign exchange reserves sustained foreign direct investment, and rising export earnings will provide an adequate buffer against possible global liquidity tapering in 2022–23.

- The economic impact of "second wave" was much smaller than that during the full lockdown phase in 2020–21, though its health impact was more severe.

- The Government of India's unique response comprised safety-nets to cushion the impact on vulnerable sections of society and the business sector, a significant increase in capital expenditure to spur growth, and supply-side reforms for a sustained long-term expansion.

- The government's flexible and multi-layered response is partly based on an "Agile" framework that uses feedback-loops, and the use of 80 high-frequency indicators (HFIs) in an environment of extreme uncertainty.

*Source:* Press Information Bureau, Govt. of India

## 1.3    Entrepreneurship and Start-up Scenario in India

India is the third largest start-up ecosystem in the world with almost 73,000 start-ups spread across 56 diverse sectors. The country has seen unprecedented growth in the number of unicorns which are over 100 now. Indian start-ups raised funding of over $42 billion in 2021 with over $11 billion funding in the first quarter of 2022.[4]

The Start-up India mission, launched on 16 January 2016, has seen tremendous success in building the start-up ecosystem of the country. There is nine times increase in the number of investors and seven times increase in the total funding for start-ups and the number of incubators each (Fig. 1.6).

Though the COVID-19 pandemic caused an economic downturn globally but it also led to a heavy increase in traffic on digital media. This resulted in opportunities for tech-based start-ups to react immediately and IT/ITeS-based companies/sectors emerged as a solution to several problems. The main sectors that emerged for start-ups during COVID-19 are digital education, fintech, health and wellbeing, shared office space, and remote working tools (please see Fig. 1.7).

Figure 1.8 shows that the total number of funding deals and funding amount both have tremendously increased for EdTech start-ups in 2021 in the country. The total number of funding deals increased from 49 in 2019 to 103 in 2020, and 165 in 2021 whereas the total funding amount increased from US$ 0.44 billion to US$ 1.4 billion, and US$ 4.7 billion during the same period.

Further, funding in the health tech sector in India also witnessed a remarkable increase during the period following COVID-19; however, it declined sharply during the pandemic. It was US$ 1000 million in 2019, declined to US$ 388 million in 2020, and increased to US$ 2100 million in 2021. This trend is shown in Figure 1.9.

**9x Increase** in Number of Investors

**7x Increase** in Total Funding of Startups

**7x Increase** in Number of Incubators

FIGURE 1.6    Start-up Ecosystem in India (2015–22)

*Source: States' Start-up Ranking 2021*

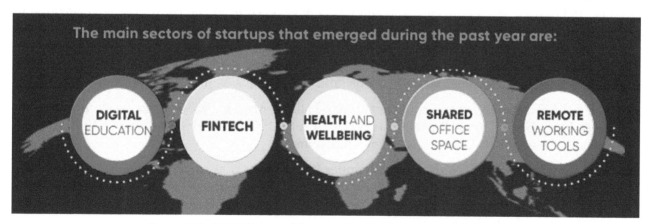

The main sectors of startups that emerged during the past year are:

DIGITAL EDUCATION    FINTECH    HEALTH AND WELLBEING    SHARED OFFICE SPACE    REMOTE WORKING TOOLS

FIGURE 1.7    Major Sector of Start-ups that Emerged During COVID-19

[4]States' Start-up Ranking 2021, Department for Promotion of Industry and Internal Trade, Ministry of Commerce and Industry, Government of India

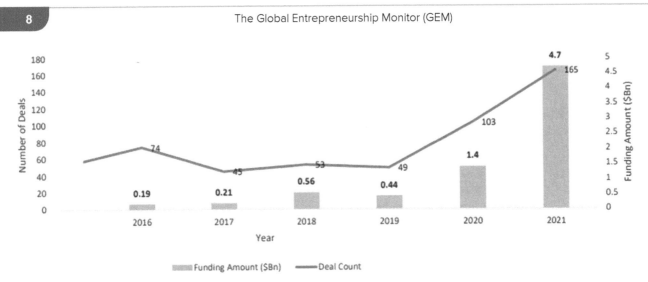

**FIGURE 1.8**    Funding Deals and Amount for EdTech Start-ups in India

*Source: States' Start-up Ranking 2021*

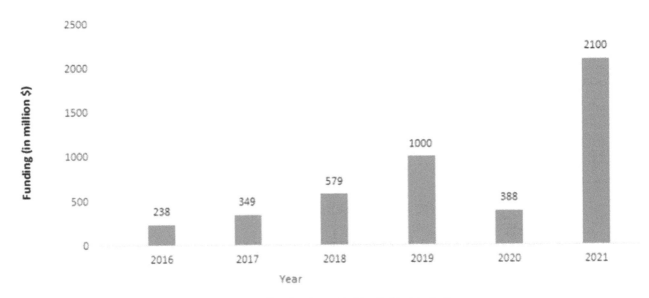

**FIGURE 1.9**    Funding Trend in Health Tech in India

*Source: Health Tech India Report 2021, Tracxn 2021*

Further, to boost entrepreneurship and the start-up ecosystem in the country, the Government of India has also been taking substantial measures. Union Budget 2022 presented the blue print of India at 75 to India at 100 with four pillars of development including inclusive development, productivity enhancement, energy transition, and climate action. Some of the major announcements for business, start-ups, and the promotion of entrepreneurship are:

- The holiday scheme for start-ups is extended till 31 March 2023 to incentivise funding for these businesses. This will enable start-ups to get a 100% tax rebate as long as their annual turnover is under Rs 25 crore in a financial year.

- A fund with blended capital raised under the co-investment model facilitated through NABARD to finance start-ups in agriculture and rural enterprises for the farm-produce value chain will be set up. Further, start-ups would support farmer-producer organisations (FPOs) and offer tech support to farmers.

- Ease of Doing Business 2.0 aims to digitize manual processes, remove overlapping compliances, and promote the integration of state- and central-level systems.

- The concessional corporate tax of 15% will be extended for another year till March 2024 for newly incorporated manufacturing enterprises.

- Promoting start-ups and extending drone support for farmers through Kisan Drones for crop assessment.

- Digital Rupee will be issued using block chain technology.

- Corporate surcharge to be reduced from 12% to 7%.

## 1.4 Future Entrepreneurship Agenda and Global Entrepreneurship Monitor (GEM) Report 2022

India is emerging as one of the most sought-after destinations for innovation, start-ups, and entrepreneurship. Some of the favorable factors for creating a business and entrepreneurship ecosystem are a huge growing market, rising technological advancements, market access, government will and support, research capabilities with increasing research infrastructure, a growing number of higher educational institutions offering programs with a focus on innovation and entrepreneurship, etc.

The Government of India is providing its full support to build a highly attractive business ecosystem in the country and has announced several packages, such as a Production-Linked Incentive (PLI) scheme for several sectors such as telecom, pharmaceuticals, automobile, among others; reduction in tax compliances, early tax benefits, availability of loans through financial institutions, setting up of start-up centers, establishing business incubators, research parks, etc. Recently, the Govt. of India announced a PLI scheme for semiconductors manufacturing worth Rs. 76,000 crores and the country's first semiconductor manufacturing plant is coming up in Gujarat by Vedanta–Foxconn.

All efforts of the government are generating results to make the country one of the most sought-after investment destinations for doing business. It is clearly reflected in India's significant improvements (ranked 130 in 2017 and 63 in 2020) in the Ease of Doing Business Ranking, published by the World Bank.

The overall improvements in the doing business ecosystem are positioning the nation as a country with a very suitable environment for entrepreneurship. The Global Entrepreneurship Monitor (GEM) 2020–21 report placed India amongst the top five economies globally to start a business, reflecting an entrepreneurial ecosystem that has improved, thanks to government initiatives such as 'Start-up India' and 'Make in India'.[5]

The GEM Research was started in 1999 and since then, it has surveyed almost four million people in more than 110 economies. The GEM Research Report for India is prepared and published by the Entrepreneurship Development Institute of India, Ahmedabad, and the GEM India Report 2021–22 has brought new facets in entrepreneurship in the country and 'Total Entrepreneurial Activity' (TEA) has reached almost its pre-pandemic level, 14.40% in 2021–22 which declined to 5.30% in 2020–21 (during the pandemic) from 15.0% in 2019–20.

---

[5]India among top 5 economies for ease of starting new business: Global survey - Business News (indiatoday.in)

# Global Entrepreneurship Monitor (GEM) Conceptual Framework

**2**

## 2.1 GEM in India

The prestigious GEM Research Project was initiated in India by the N.S. Raghavan Centre for Entrepreneurial Learning (NSRCEL) at IIM-Bangalore in 2001. Following the successful accomplishment of GEM India research project in 2001, it was again undertaken in 2002. Back then, the GEM Research model was in its nascent stage and the "Assessment of Entrepreneurial Activity" in the country was a new concept. Prof. Mathew J. Manimala (NSRCEL-IIM-B) conducted GEM India survey during 2001 and 2002 under GEM Research Project, and delivered research work in the form of two annual reports. Subsequently, during 2006–08, a team of Prof. I.M. Pandey, Prof. Ashutosh Bhupatkar, and Prof. Janki Raman from the Pearl School of Business-Gurgaon conducted GEM India study. The surveys were conducted over 3 years and the data were featured in GEM Global Report 2006, 2007, and 2008. However, the GEM India team could not publish the National Report during the same period. In the succeeding years (2008–11) GEM India study was not undertaken.

In 2011, with an aim to continue with the GEM India Study, the three institutions, that is, Entrepreneurship Development Institute of India-Ahmedabad, Wadhwani Centre for Entrepreneurship Development, Indian School of Business, Hyderabad, and Institute of Management Technology-Ghaziabad; formed the GEM India Consortium 2012–15. As per the stipulated requirements, the "GEM India" consortium conducted research studies in 2012, 2013, and 2014. The research results of the study conducted in 2013, were featured in the GEM National Report-2013 and GEM National Report-2014. After 3 years, "GEM India 2012–15" consortium was reconstituted. The three institutions (i.e., EDII-Ahmedabad, Jammu and Kashmir Entrepreneurship Development Institute of India-JKEDI, and Centre for Entrepreneurship Development Madhya Pradesh-CEDMAP) agreed to conduct the GEM study in a time-bound manner, which was in line with the GEM Global schedule. This team could produce GEM India National Reports 2015/16, 2016/17, and 2017/18. Further, the EDII, as the GEM India Lead Institution has continued the Annual Cycle of GEM Research Study and brought National Reports in 2019, 2020, and 2021.

The present "GEM India Team" comprises the Entrepreneurship Development Institute of India which is the Lead Institution and the Secretariat of the GEM India Team, Prof. Sunil Shukla (Director General, EDII), is the National Team Leader for GEM India Study.

## 2.2 Income Groups and Participating Economies of GEM Research

This annual GEM India draws comparisons between "Level C" economies that participated in GEM's 2021 research. For GEM, entrepreneurial activity or entrepreneurship is the act of starting and running a new business, that is, not just thinking about it, or intending to start, but expending resources to get a new business off the ground (GEM 2021/2022).

GEM global report 2021/22 has provided detailed information regarding participating economies, regions, and income levels. There are 50 economies in this latest survey that belong to three income groups. In the 2021/2022 Global Report, GEM has continued to use World Bank data but has defined its own income boundaries in order to achieve a more even spread of participating economies, and hence more meaningful comparisons (GEM 2021/22).

Table 2.1 outlines the GEM-participating economies, categorized by GEM into three income levels, using World Bank GDP per capita data as follows:

- **Level A:** Economies with a Gross Domestic Product (GDP) per capita of more than $40,000;

TABLE 2.1   Economies in GEM 2021, Classified by Income ($GDP per Capita)

| Level C <br> <$20,000 | Level B <br> >$20,000<$40,000 | Level A <br> >$40,000 |
|---|---|---|
| Brazil | Belarus | Canada |
| Colombia | Chile | Finland |
| Dominican Republic | Croatia | France |
| Egypt | Cyprus | Germany |
| Guatemala | Greece | Ireland |
| India | Hungary | Israel |
| Iran | Kazakhstan | Italy |
| Jamaica | Latvia | Japan |
| Mexico | Lithuania | Luxembourg |
| Morocco | Oman | Netherlands |
| South Africa | Panama | Norway |
| Sudan | Poland | Qatar |
| | Romania | Republic of Korea |
| | Russian Federation | Saudi Arabia |
| | Slovak Republic | Sweden |
| | Slovenia | Switzerland |
| | Spain | United Arab Emirates |
| | Turkey | United Kingdom |
| | Uruguay | United States |
| | Belarus | |
| | Chile | |
| | Croatia | |
| | Cyprus | |
| | Greece | |
| | Hungary | |
| | Kazakhstan | |

*Source: GEM 2021/2022*

- **Level B:** Economies with a GDP per capita of between £20,000 and $40,000;
- **Level C:** Economies with a GDP per capita of less than $20,000.

Level A includes economies from northern Europe, East Asia, and North America, plus three Gulf states, while a majority of Level B economies are from Southern or Eastern Europe. Level C is dominated by economies from Latin America, the Caribbean, and Africa. These categorizations will be used in the comparison and analysis of data.

## 2.3   The GEM Conceptual Framework

The societal, economical, and political context of entrepreneurship has a great impact on generating an entrepreneurial environment in any economy. The conceptual framework helps to understand the multifaceted phenomenon of entrepreneurship which includes innovation in products and services, business renewal, job creation, economic expansion, and social and environmental implications of business. The GEM framework (Fig. 2.1) and the data analysis help to understand that the entrepreneur is not the only entitlement to economic growth but it is the environment (ecosystem) that together generates a promising culture of entrepreneurship. An ecosystem of different determinants with individual attributes results in a more conducive environment for new ventures and new opportunities to bloom.

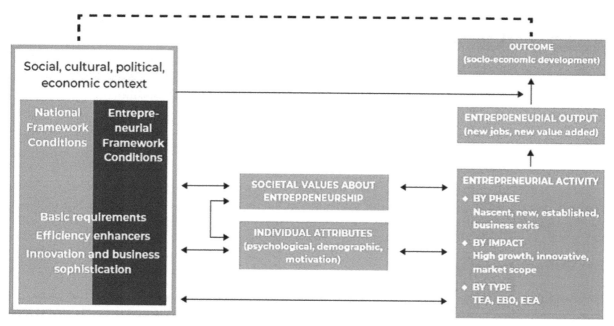

FIGURE 2.1    The GEM Conceptual Framework

**Source:** *GEM Global Report 2021-22*

The level of entrepreneurial activity is the result of an assessment of entrepreneurial opportunities and their entrepreneurial potential (i.e., motivation and capacity). Recognition of opportunities and entrepreneurial potential is influenced by both entrepreneurial framework conditions and national framework conditions. While entrepreneurial framework conditions are also influenced by the general framework conditions within a nation. The National Framework Conditions reflect the level of economic development. According to GEM, the entrepreneurial framework condition consists of the following factors:

- **Finance:** The availability of financial resources, equity debt for small and medium-sized enterprises (SMEs) (including grants and subsidies), and the extent to which taxes or regulations are either size-neutral or encourage SMEs.

- **Government policies:** The presence and quality of direct programmers to assist new and growing firms at all levels of government (national, regional, and municipal).

- **Entrepreneurial education and training:** The extent to which training in creating or managing SMEs is incorporated within the education and training system at all levels (primary, secondary, and post-school).

- **R&D transfer:** The extent to which national research and development will lead to new commercial opportunities and is available to SMEs.

- **Commercial and legal infrastructure:** The presence of property rights and commercial, accounting, and other legal services and institutions that support or promote SMEs.

- **Entry regulation:** It contains two components: (1) Market dynamics: the level of change in markets from year to year and (2) Market openness: the extent to which new firms are free to enter the existing markets.

- **Physical infrastructure and services:** Ease of access to physical resources, that is, communication, utilities, transportation, land, or space at a price that does not discriminate against SMEs.

- **Cultural and social norms:** The extent to which social and cultural norms encourage or allow actions leading to new business methods or activities that can potentially increase personal wealth and income.

## 2.4   Social Values Toward Entrepreneurship

It includes how society values entrepreneurship as the right career choice; if entrepreneurs have a high social status; and how media attention to entrepreneurship is contributing (or not) to the development of national entrepreneurial culture.

### 2.4.1   Individual Attributes

It includes several demographic factors (gender, age, and geography), psychological factors (perceived capabilities, perceived opportunities, and fear of failure), and motivational aspects (necessity-based vs. opportunity-based venturing, improvement-driven venturing, etc.).

### 2.4.2   Entrepreneurial Activity

Entrepreneurial activity is defined according to the ventures' lifecycle phases (nascent, new venture, established venture, and discontinuation), the types of activity (high growth, innovation, and internationalization), and the sector of the activity (Total Early-stage Entrepreneurial Activity or TEA, Social Entrepreneurial Activity or SEA, and Employee Entrepreneurial Activity or EEA [Fig. 2.2]).

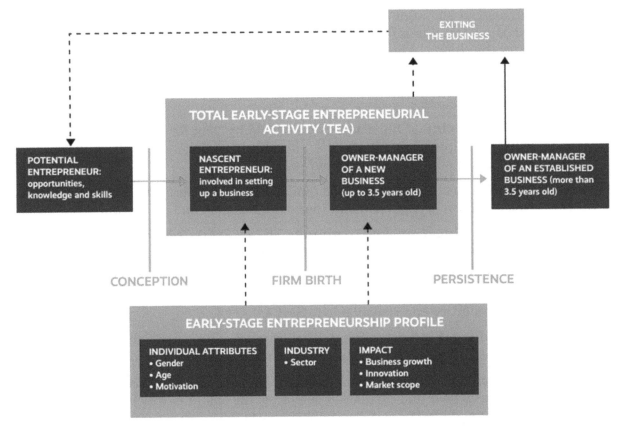

**FIGURE 2.2**   Entrepreneurship Phases and GEM Entrepreneurship Indicators

*Source: GEM Global Report 2021–22*

## 2.5 GEM Operational Definitions

- **TEA:** Percentage of individuals aged 18–64 who are either nascent entrepreneurs or owner-manager of a new business.

- **Nascent entrepreneurship rate:** Percentage of individuals aged 18–64 who are currently nascent entrepreneurs, that is, actively involved in setting up a business they will own or co-own; this business has not paid salaries, wages, or any other payments to the owners for more than 3 months.

- **New business ownership rate:** Percentage of individuals aged 18–64 who are currently an owner-manager of a new business, that is, owning and managing a running business that has paid salaries, wages, or any other payments to the owners for more than 3 months but not more than 42 months.

### 2.5.1 Characteristics of Early-stage Entrepreneurial Activity

- **High-growth expectation early-stage entrepreneurial activity:** The percentage of early-stage entrepreneurs (as defined above) who expect to employ at least 20 people 5 years from now.

- **New product-market-oriented early-stage entrepreneurial activity:** The percentage of early-stage entrepreneurs (as defined above) who report that their product or service is new to at least some customers and not many businesses offer the same product or service.

- **International-oriented early-stage entrepreneurial activity:** The percentage of early-stage entrepreneurs (as defined above) who report that at least 25% of their customers are from foreign countries.

- **Established business ownership rate:** The percentage of individuals aged 18–64 years who are currently an owner-manager of an established business, that is, owning and managing a running business that has paid salaries, wages, or any other payments to the owners for more than 42 months.

- **Business discontinuation rate:** The percentage of individuals aged 18–64 years who in the past 12 months have discontinued a business, either by selling, shutting down, or otherwise discontinuing an owner/management relationship with the business. It may be noted that it is NOT a measure of business failure rates.

### 2.5.2 Individual Attributes of a Potential Entrepreneur

- **Perceived opportunities:** Percentage of the 18–64 population who see good opportunities to start a firm in the area where they live.

- **Perceived capabilities:** Percentage of the 18–64 population who believe they have the required skills and knowledge to start a business.

- **Entrepreneurial intentions:** Percentage of the 18–64 population (individuals involved in any stage of entrepreneurial activity excluded) who intend to start a business within 3 years.

- **Fear of failure rate:** Percentage of the 18–64 population with perceived opportunities who also indicate that fear of failure would prevent them from setting up a business.

## 2.6   The GEM Methodology

The GEM methodology is unique due to its concentration on youth rather than businesses. It depends more on the quality and characteristics of the youth it studies than on enterprises for which data is available globally. This is important because the attitudes, activities, and ambitions of people influence the entrepreneurial process in a society. An economy needs entrepreneurs to grow and sustain at every stage in that some are starting a new business and have established a business and sustained into maturity. The GEM survey in every participant country is held in two different phases: Adult Population Survey (APS) and National Expert Survey (NES). The purpose of GEM is to find empirical answers to the following questions:

- Does the level of entrepreneurial activity vary between countries, and if so, to what extent?
- Does the level of entrepreneurial activity affect a country's rate of economic growth and prosperity?
- What makes a country entrepreneurial?
- What kind of policies may enhance the national level of entrepreneurial activity?

## 2.7   APS in India

The APS asks a nationally representative sample of more than 2000 adults about their attitudes, motivations, ambitions, and activities using the standard global gem questionnaire. Results and surveys are then checked by GEM global and later approved based on quality and cross-checks. APS in every country and India especially brings out the relevant information to the informal economy, which is very crucial to the developing world. It helps analyze diverse sets of economic activities, enterprises, and jobs that are neither regulated nor protected by the state. With unaccounted informal businesses, a country may overlook taxes and people may not comply with labor laws. As the GEM survey is random and distributed throughout the population, these activities are easy to be captured and monitored as a part of the entrepreneurship evolution.

A stratified random sampling method is used to select cities or villages across the country. Further, a city/village is divided into four to five strata and the selection of a certain number of survey starting points within each city/ village is ensured. Moreover, with the help of the Kish Grid method, households and adults were identified for the survey. Rather than selecting the respondents directly from the population, a two-stage sampling method is used. Hence, after the identification of the household, the eligible age group was listed in descending order by age and an eligible respondent is identified by the Next Birthday method. If a selected person was not available at the time of the initial visit, at least three more visits were made before moving to another household. In all, 3252 respondents aged between 18 and 64 years were included in the survey.

TABLE 2.2   Regional Distribution of APS

| Region | Frequency | Percent |
| --- | --- | --- |
| North | 1000 | 30.8 |
| West | 797 | 24.5 |
| South | 824 | 25.3 |
| East | 631 | 19.4 |
| Total | 3252 | 100.0 |

*Source: Based on GEM India Survey 2021/22*

Apart from regional representation (Table 2.2), an effort was also made to ensure appropriate representation on the basis of gender and location, that is, male/female and urban/rural, respectively (please see Table 2.3 and 2.4). For this purpose, appropriate weight was decided on the basis of various criteria.

TABLE 2.3    Rural/Urban Distribution

| Location | Frequency | Percent | Frequency | Percent |
|---|---|---|---|---|
| | Unweighted | | Weighted | |
| Urban | 2156 | 66.3 | 1090 | 33.5 |
| Rural | 1096 | 33.7 | 2162 | 66.5 |
| Total | 3252 | 100.0 | 3252 | 100 |

*Source:* Based on GEM India Survey 2021/22

TABLE 2.4    Gender Distribution

| Gender | Frequency | Percent | Frequency | Percent |
|---|---|---|---|---|
| | Unweighted | | Weighted | |
| Male | 1694 | 52.1 | 1664 | 51.2 |
| Female | 1558 | 47.9 | 1588 | 48.8 |
| Total | 3252 | 100.0 | 3252 | |

*Source:* Based on GEM India Survey 2021/22

## 2.8   NES in India

The second source of the GEM data is the National Expert Survey (NES) conducted via email on the state of entrepreneurship in the country with 72 national-level experts from both public and private sectors. The information was collected with the help of a standardized questionnaire provided under the global GEM project. The national level of experts was selected for their expertise based on the "entrepreneurial framework conditions." They are equipped with rich perspectives about not only their respective professions but also entrepreneurship. The experts are asked to estimate the degree to which each factor of the entrepreneurship ecosystem is applicable to India.

In all, 72 national experts were identified, approached, and requested for data provision. The average work experience of experts was 9.8 years and ranged between 1 and 30 years. The profile of experts and their areas of specialization is given in Tables 2.5 and 2.6, respectively.

Expert specialization included experts' opinions from entrepreneurs, investors, finance specialists, policymakers, business and support service providers. Also included experts from education and entrepreneurship research. The number of participants in these fields differs and education level also varies.

TABLE 2.5    Experts' Specialization (includes Multiple Responses)

| Sl. No. | Specialization | No. | Percentage |
|---|---|---|---|
| 1 | Entrepreneur | 30 | 41.7 |
| 2 | Investor, Financer, Banker | 9 | 12.5 |
| 3 | Policymaker | 6 | 8.3 |
| 4 | Business and Support Services Provider | 24 | 33.3 |
| 5 | Educator, Teacher, Entrepreneurship Researcher | 31 | 43.1 |

*Source:* Based on GEM India Survey 2021/22

The expert as reflected in Table 2.6 included people with a qualification up to Ph.D. Some are vocational professionals and university college academics. The experts also include people with Ph.D and researchers in the entrepreneurship field.

TABLE 2.6   Experts' Education

| Sl. No. | Educational Qualification | Frequency | Percent |
|---------|--------------------------|-----------|---------|
| 1 | Secondary | 1 | 1.4 |
| 2 | Vocational Professional | 7 | 9.7 |
| 3 | University/college | 30 | 41.7 |
| 4 | MA, Ph.D. | 34 | 47.2 |
| 5 | Total | 72 | 100.0 |

*Source: Based on GEM India Survey 2021/22*

The experts in the NES survey are classified into the male and female categories as well. In the below table, it is clear that there were 15 female and 57 male experts to provide their opinion for the Indian national expert survey.

# Measuring Entrepreneurship Activity in India

**3**

## 3.1 Overview

This chapter highlights the yearly trends and current situation through data points obtained from the survey of adults in the country. This adult population survey (APS) identifies the entrepreneurial potential and confidence of the population in the entrepreneurial initiative taken by the government and the individuals themselves. Adult population survey is conducted by all the national teams involved in the year's reporting and survey of adults in their respective countries. Around 47 countries participate in the APS every year and more than 2000 adults on average are surveyed. This survey is conducted among adults, entrepreneurs, students, nascent entrepreneurs, aspiring entrepreneurs, and others.

## 3.2 Components of Analysis

In Table 3.1 (GEM India Snapshot), an overview of changes can be seen for the duration of 3 years from 2019–20 to 2021–22. This chapter explains the total entrepreneurial activity (TEA)

TABLE 3.1   GEM India Snapshot

| Total Entrepreneurial Activity | Value (%) | Rank |
|---|---|---|
| **TEA 2021–22** | 14.4 | 18/47 |
| TEA 2020–21 | 5.3 | 39/43 |
| TEA 2019–20 | 15.0 | 13/50 |
| The established business ownership **rate (2021–22)** | 8.5 | 13/47 |
| Entrepreneurial Employee Activity—EEA | 0.1 | 43/43 |

| Gender Equity | Value (%) | |
|---|---|---|
| Male TEA | 16.3 (7.9 in 2020–21) | |
| Female TEA | 12.3 (2.6 in 2020–21) | |

| Motivation | % of TEA | Rank/47 |
|---|---|---|
| Make a difference in the world | 75.9 | 3 |
| Build great wealth | 73.4 | 14 |
| Continue family tradition | 74.3 | 1 |
| Earn living because jobs are scarce | 91.5 | 2 |
| Make a difference in the world | 75.9 | 3 |

| Motivation | Age Group (18–34) | Age Group (35–64) |
|---|---|---|
| Make a difference in the world | 78.1 | 76.7 |
| Build great wealth | 70.4 | 71.6 |
| Continue family tradition | 70.2 | 78.4 |
| Earn living because jobs are scarce | 90.9 | 92.1 |
| Make a difference in the world | 78.1 | 76.7 |

| Attitudes and Perceptions | Value (%) | Rank/47 |
|---|---|---|
| Perceived opportunity | 83.4 | 2 |
| Perceived capability | 86.0 | 4 |
| Fear of failure | 54.1 | 2 |
| Entrepreneurial intention | 18.1 | 21 |
| Easy to start a business | 82.2 | 4 |

*Source: GEM India Survey 2021/22*

in the country. It provides male–female comparison, a motivation comparison of age groups and TEA, and TEA comparisons among various regions within India. The chapter also discusses job-creation expectations, innovation, and motivations. The data further highlight entrepreneurial motivation and its value among youth and entrepreneurs.

Discussions for other data points like TEA in India and its comparison with countries in the low-income group (whose per capita income is less than $20,000) are a part of the analysis. The proportion of entrepreneurial activity in India in various ways can be seen in this chapter.

Table 3.1 consists of the current year's most important data points. The results shown under multiple headings, such as self-perception (individual perception), societal values concern to the social outlook of the respondents, and entrepreneurial activity as well as gender equality-based analysis and other are parts of the societal or a general outlook of the society. The motivational index is another important development in the Global Entrepreneurship Monitor (GEM) report this year. This index will help to measure and analyze things more harmoniously.

## 3.3    Attitudes and Perception

Individual perceptions reflect the intentions toward a certain goal. In the GEM terminology, it reflects the intent toward business opportunities for starting a business. The data in Table 3.2 reflects that 63.1% of the country's population perceives that they know someone who has recently started a new business. This data reflects that majority of the population has awareness of starting a new business by someone they know. This helps them widen their understanding and know the importance of opening up new businesses in the country.

TABLE 3.2    Attitudes and Perception to Start a Business in India

| Attitudes and Perceptions | Value % | GEM Rank/50 |
|---|---|---|
| Know someone who has started a new business | 63.1 | 11 |
| Good opportunities to start a business in my area | 83.4 | 2 |
| It is easy to start a business | 82.2 | 4 |
| Personally, have the skills and knowledge | 86.0 | 4 |
| Fear of failure (opportunity) | 54.1 | 2 |
| Entrepreneurial intentions | 18.1 | 21 |

*Source: GEM India Survey 2021–22*

The majority of the country's adult population perceives that there are good business opportunities in the area they live. While this reflects the notion of the population, the intention to take these opportunities has been seen as less than one-fourth of the same percentage. More than 83% of the population responds that opportunities are available in their area. This reflects the positive intentions of adults toward entrepreneurship.

The result indicates that 82.2% of youth perceive that it is easy to start a business in India. This easy-to-start business greatly depends upon the efforts of the government toward ease of doing business and start-up. The percentage of opportunities available and the ease to start a business are nearly at the same percentage value. This highlights that individuals are highly positive about starting a new business venture.

Another important data point in this survey is the perception of skill and knowledge for starting a business among the adult population of India. The data show that nearly 86% of the population is confident that they possess the skills and knowledge to start a new business. This data is reflected in the previous data points as well, however, the same is not reflected in the fear of failure among these individuals. The fear of failure in this data table reflects that nearly 54% of the population fears starting a new business due to many known and unknown reasons. This is a three-point percentage dip as compared to last year's 57%. Fear of failure is an important perception and keeps individuals away from starting their new business even when the person possesses all the resources, has great skills, and the external environment is supportive. The fear of failure is basically attached to the mindset and it needs great effort to overcome the fear of failure and also leads to early failure if the same individuals start a new business. Fear of failure is very relevant to the middle- and lower-income classes of society. As entrepreneurship is a task of risk and uncertainty, this statement helps us understand this particular trait among Indians. Fear of failure is inflicted on individuals either naturally or due to social perceptions regarding business.

## 3.4  The COVID Impact

The impact of COVID has led to decreased household income among 90% of the surveyed population of India, which is the second-highest impact as compared to other countries. Though, 77.6% population would choose entrepreneurship opportunities to cope with this situation. It is important to mention here that in all 59.3% of youth reported that they have used more digital technology to sell the product.

TABLE 3.3   Impact of COVID

| COVID Related | | |
|---|---|---|
| | % Adults | Rank/47 |
| Pandemic has led household income to decrease* | 90.8 | 2 |
| | % TEA | Rank/47 |
| Use more digital technology to sell products or services | 59.3 | 17 |
| Pursue new opportunities due to pandemic | 77.6 | 1 |

*Source: GEM India Survey 2021–22*

## 3.5  Male–female Attitudes and Perceptions

Among the five variables, surprisingly as in contrast to the last year, the fear of failure among females is lesser among the males. When 56.2% of male respondents express fear of failure, only 51.7% of female respondents depict the same. In all other variables, males are leading by a few percentage points while in fear of failure women are seen as less fearful to start a new business.

The fifth variable, which is "Entrepreneurial Intentions," is also at the same percentage points (18.2%) that reflect equal readiness among both genders. It shows that while intentions can be the same, it is other variables in perceptions' and attitudes' variance, which may lead to a change in actions for entrepreneurial activity.

In the data, it can be seen that males are leading with the percentage for perceived opportunity and more than 84% of males and 82% of females perceive there are good opportunities in their area.

Another important data point is the knowledge and skill required to start a new business among males and females. The data shows that 90.2% of males and 81.5% of females perceive that they possess the required skills to start a new business in India.

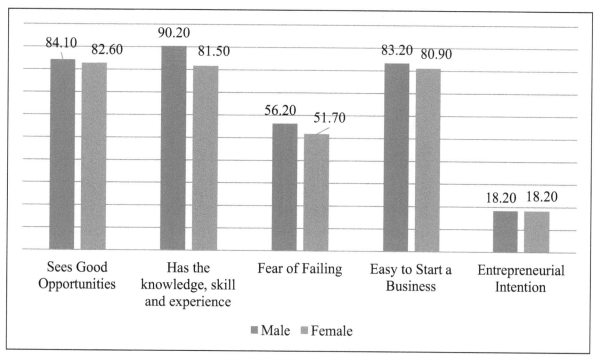

FIGURE 3.1    Attitudes and Perception of Males and Females in India

*Source: GEM India Survey 2021–22*

Change of attitude is important with respect to the "fear of failure." Both males and females depict the intention in other statements but do not want to start only because they fear they will fail in the business they start. An important generalization from this figure is that both males and females perceive high opportunity, skill, and ease to start a business but a higher percentage believe they will fail in their attempt. So there is a need to create an environment where failure is not seen as a stigma and particularly in entrepreneurship it is used and understood as a fruitful exercise.

## 3.6    Attitudes and Perception: A Comparison of BRICS Countries

The graphical representation in Figure 3.2 provides a data comparison of attitudes and perceptions among the four countries of BRICS—Brazil, Russian Federation, India, and South Africa. It is important to mention here that China has not participated in this survey. Among these countries, India shows a high percentage to be perceiving good opportunities and others. However, the data also reflects that fear of failure has increased higher than in other countries. The existence of fear of failure keeps the country's population away from grabbing new opportunities in the entrepreneurship field. India leads with 86% of the population perceiving that they possess the knowledge to start a business in their country. This is followed by South Africa where 69.7% of respondents believe they possess enough knowledge to start a business. The data also reveal that more than 54.1% of Indians believe that they have a fear of failure to start a business in the country. The data also reveal that fear of failure is lowest among the Brazilians. Only 45.1% of Brazilians perceive fear of failure and it is an important statistic to analyze here.

Though India fares the highest among all variables except "Entrepreneurial Intention," it is clear that owing to highest degree of fear of failure, which is 54%, India's Entrepreneurial Intention (18.1%) is also showing a downturn with a huge variance between Brazil, which is as high as 53%.

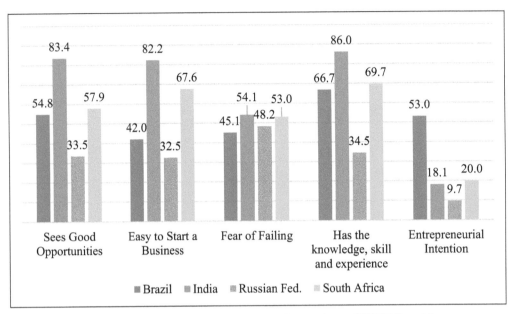

FIGURE 3.2   Attitudes and Perception: A Comparison of BRICS Countries

*Source: GEM India Survey 2021–22*

## 3.7   Attitudes and Perception: A Comparison in Low-Income Countries

Even if we compare India with other "Low-Income Countries" such as Brazil, Columbia, Dominic Republic, Egypt, Guatemala, Iran, Morocco, South Africa, and Sudan, India scores highest among all variables except "having the knowledge, skill and experience." India ranks second after Sudan showing the same as high as 88.1%. India is at the lowest position in terms of "Entrepreneurial Intention" and Egypt scores the highest on this parameter.

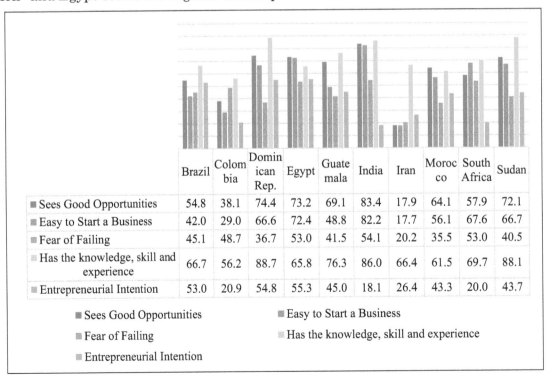

| | Brazil | Colombia | Dominican Rep. | Egypt | Guatemala | India | Iran | Morocco | South Africa | Sudan |
|---|---|---|---|---|---|---|---|---|---|---|
| ■ Sees Good Opportunities | 54.8 | 38.1 | 74.4 | 73.2 | 69.1 | 83.4 | 17.9 | 64.1 | 57.9 | 72.1 |
| ■ Easy to Start a Business | 42.0 | 29.0 | 66.6 | 72.4 | 48.8 | 82.2 | 17.7 | 56.1 | 67.6 | 66.7 |
| ■ Fear of Failing | 45.1 | 48.7 | 36.7 | 53.0 | 41.5 | 54.1 | 20.2 | 35.5 | 53.0 | 40.5 |
| ■ Has the knowledge, skill and experience | 66.7 | 56.2 | 88.7 | 65.8 | 76.3 | 86.0 | 66.4 | 61.5 | 69.7 | 88.1 |
| ■ Entrepreneurial Intention | 53.0 | 20.9 | 54.8 | 55.3 | 45.0 | 18.1 | 26.4 | 43.3 | 20.0 | 43.7 |

■ Sees Good Opportunities                    ■ Easy to Start a Business

■ Fear of Failing                            ■ Has the knowledge, skill and experience

■ Entrepreneurial Intention

FIGURE 3.3   Attitudes and Perception: A Comparison in Low-Income Countries

*Source: GEM India Survey 2021–22*

Fear of failure is the lowest in Iran. Iran scores below average on other variables and it seems for this reason its' "Entrepreneurial Intention" is also not very high in spite of "fear of failure" being the lowest.

## 3.8 Region-wise Perceptions and Attitudes

Every year a region-wise data analysis is done to understand the data points from all four regions of the country. The data points highlight that samples must be collected from all the parts and regions of the country to highlight the country's regional perspective. A total of 83.4% population in India perceives an opportunity to start a business.

The northern part of India scores highest in the perception of "sees good opportunity" at 90.6% followed by the southern region at 83.2%, the eastern at 80.0%, and the western region at 76.8%. There are visible regional differences among these variables and it can be seen that respondents from North India are more inclined to be entrepreneurs in the country. Perceived capabilities are highest in South India followed by West India and then by North India. The data also show that fear of failure is highest among South India and followed by North, East, and least found in the western part of the country. People in North India (90.8%) believe that it is easy to start a new business in their region followed by people in South, West, and East.

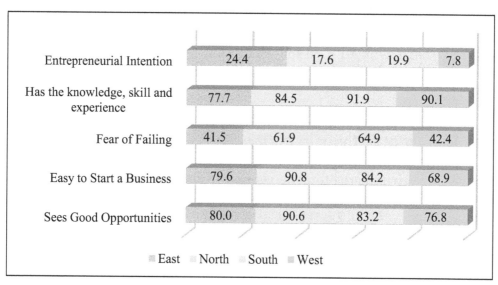

**FIGURE 3.4** Perception and Attitudes: A Comparison of the Indian Region

*Source: GEM India Survey 2021–22*

Entrepreneurship is praised in certain regions and certain regions meagerly prioritize it. The typical reason for lower TEA in one region and higher in other may be explained by the fact that the western region of the country is more entrepreneurial, more business exists there, industries and work environment is suitable while other regions are half mountainous, or poorer than other regions. There may be many causes for the less involvement of regions in entrepreneurial activity but entrepreneurship is growing in the country and it is flourishing in the facts discussed in the GEM India snapshots.

## 3.9 Attitude and Perception: Urban Rural Comparison

On one hand, the surveyed population in the urban segment has the highest perception in terms of having the knowledge, skill, and experience, having high entrepreneurial intentions but at the

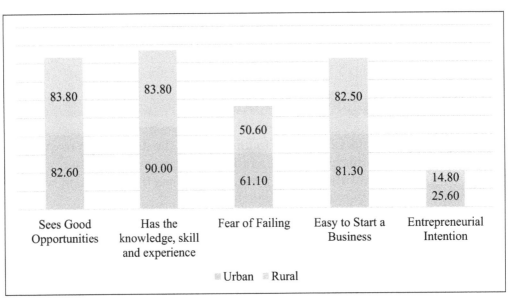

FIGURE 3.5   Attitude and Perception: Urban–Rural Comparison

*Source: GEM India Survey 2020–21*

same time having the highest percentage of "fear of failure" as compared to the rural population surveyed. On the other hand, the rural population surveyed has the highest perception of seeing good opportunities and ease to start a business. The fear of failure in the rural segment is 50.6% as compared to the urban having 61%. In spite of this low fear of failure in the urban segment, the entrepreneurial intention is low at 14.8% as compared to rural having a higher entrepreneurial intention at 25.6%.

## 3.10   Entrepreneurial Activity in India

Total entrepreneurial activity is the total percentage of the population involved in new business or existing business in the country. Majorly in this section, the following three are discussed; TEA, business ownership, and entrepreneurial employee activity. Data also identify important nuances for economies where the demographic dividend is the evident impact is seen. In India, every year data is collected to identify entrepreneurship activity among various age groups.

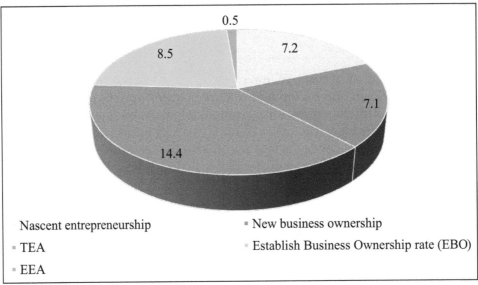

FIGURE 3.6   TEA, EBA, and EEA in India

*Source: GEM India Survey 2021–22*

Figure 3.6 provides unique data points to understand entrepreneurial activity in the country in detail. The first data point nascent entrepreneurs in this pie chart highlights those people who have recently started or have not finished three years. The data shows that 7.2% of the surveyed individuals are involved in some kind of new business and it is very low if compared to the perception of opportunity and ease of business in the country.

Another important data point in this table relates to new business owners. The data highlights that 7.1% of the surveyed individuals are claiming to be new business owners.

Entrepreneurial employee activity is also an important perspective in this analysis. Data identifies that only 0.5% of adults in the country perceive that they are contributing to entrepreneurial activity in the country. India ranks 18th under TEA. It stands at 13th rank under the variable of EBO, that is, Established Business Ownership, and 35th under the variable of Employee Entrepreneurial activity.

## 3.11  Region-wise Total Entrepreneurial Activity (TEA)

The total early-stage Entrepreneurial Activity of India is 14.4% as shown earlier, which further can be studied under the classification of gender as well as different parts of the country. The data presented in Figure 3.7 indicate that TEA varies within Indian regions. The difference is majorly due to the difference in the economic status of the states as well as the entrepreneurial ecosystem in the respective states. Entrepreneurship is praised in certain regions and certain regions meagerly prioritize it. The typical reason for lower TEA in one region and higher in other may be explained by the fact that the western region of the country is more entrepreneurial, more businesses exist there, industries and work environment are suitable while other regions are half mountainous, or poorer than other regions. As per Figure 3.7, the western part of India scores highest at 24.5% of TEA for the nation. This is followed by the South at 12.2%, the East at 11.8%, and the North at 10.6%.

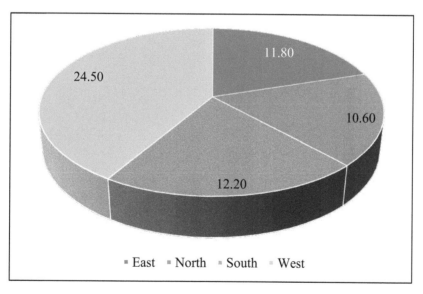

**FIGURE 3.7**   Region-wise Total Entrepreneurship Activities

*Source: GEM India Survey 2021–22*

The findings of this report also reveal that the highest rate of TEA is in the western part of the country at 29.8% among males. The lowest rate of TEA is found among females in the eastern part of the country. It means that 29.8% of the male respondents from the western region reported that they are involved in some kind of business in their respective region.

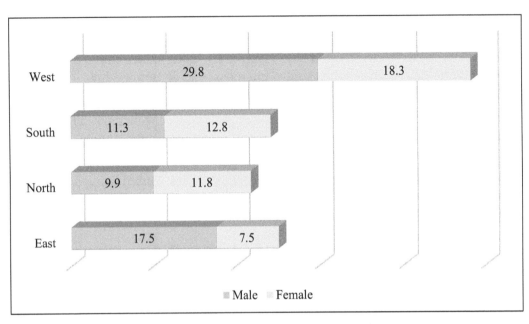

FIGURE 3.8    Total Early-Stage Entrepreneurial Activity: Region-Wise and Gender-Wise

*Source:* GEM India Survey 2021/22

## 3.12    TEA in Low-Income Countries of GEM

As seen in Figure 3.9, among the males, Morocco scores the least TEA at 5.9% whereas among the females, Egypt scores the least TEA at 5.7%. The highest TEA among males is 40.9% in Sudan and among females, it is 43.8% in the Dominican Republic. Overall, the data reflect that the highest percentage among low-income countries is seen among the female respondents of the Dominican Republic. India stands far behind this as compared to the 10 countries under this classification. The male TEA is only 16.3% and the female TEA is only 12.3%.

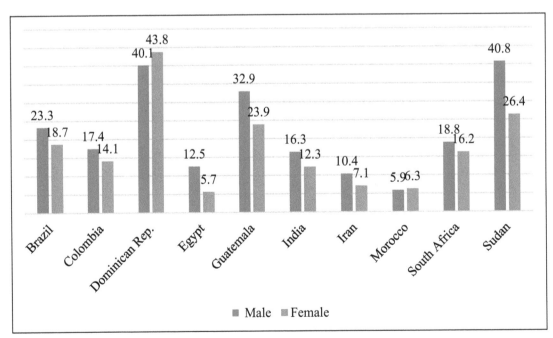

FIGURE 3.9    TEA of Low-Income Countries and Gender-Wise Comparison

*Source:* GEM India Survey 2021–22

## 3.13 TEA in BRICS Countries

As shown in Figure 3.10, a comparison of four countries is given which are Brazil, India, South Africa, and Russian Federation. As is evident, Brazil is in the top position in comparison with the remaining three countries.

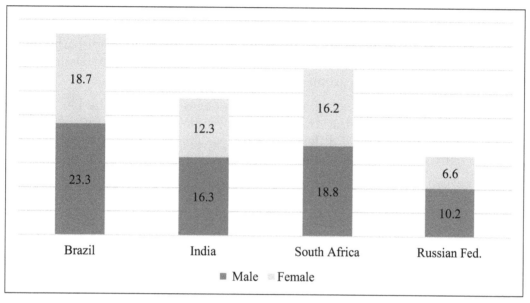

FIGURE 3.10    TEA of BRICS Countries

*Source: GEM India Survey 2021–22*

## 3.14 Age Group and Education-Wise TEA in India

Figure 3.11 depicts the age-group-wise and education-wise comparison of TEA in India. As per this representation, it is evident that there is not much difference between the age-groups TEA, which is around 14% while Indian graduates pursue entrepreneurship more than non-graduates or less educated surveyed population.

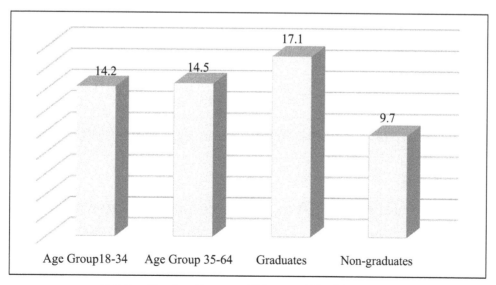

FIGURE 3.11    Age Group and Education-Wise TEA in India

*Source: GEM India Survey 2021–22*

## 3.15    Age-Group-Wise TEA in Low-Income Countries

The data for the age group 18–34 years shows that only 14.2% of the population is involved in any kind of entrepreneurial activity in India this year. For the age group, 35–64 years data show that only 14.5% of the respondents are involved in entrepreneurship of any kind in the country. There has been a halt and only a few people could overcome the pandemic and its long-lasting effects.

The age factor is highly evident in countries like Guatemala where the variance among surveyed age groups is seen to be 7% followed by a variance of 3% in Egypt between both age groups. In the age group of 18–34 years, the highest rate of TEA at 41% is seen in the Dominican Republic and with lowest in Egypt in the age group of 35–64, which is at 7.4%.

India in this age group has again scored lower than other countries in the list. The confidence has decreased and people are staying away from the same. Here it is important to say that entrepreneurship is low and high in different countries. This confirms that old people possess more sources and networks to start a business in comparison to young aged 18–34 years in some countries.

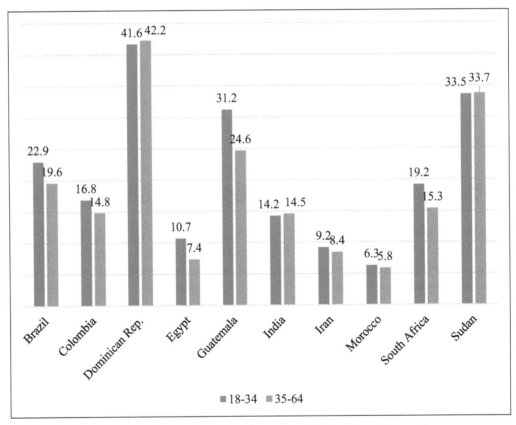

**FIGURE 3.12**    TEA of Low-Income Countries with Age-Group Comparison

*Source: GEM India Survey 2021–22*

## 3.16    Education Level-Wise TEA in Low-Income Countries

As shown in Figure 3.13, the highest number of graduates in the Dominican Republic are involved in entrepreneurship, also there is not much difference between the rate of graduates and non-graduates both involved in entrepreneurship in Dominican Republic. This is followed by Sudan with not much of a variance between both graduates and non-graduates. Graduates in India are more occupied in entrepreneurship than non-graduates.

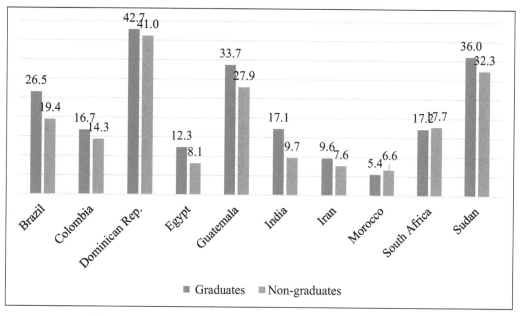

FIGURE 3.13 Education Level-Wise TEA in Low-Income Countries

**Source:** *GEM India Survey 2021–22*

It is important to mention here that the entrepreneurship measurement mentioned above includes the organizational lifecycle approach, that is, nascent, new business, established business, or nascent entrepreneurs.

## 3.17 Business Exit and Discontinuation

The business exit is a critical factor for looking into prospects and it is vital for the entrepreneurship development of a country as well. Business exits and TEA both vary in different economies. There are many reasons to exit a business. Economic conditions, personal, and finance are major reasons for discontinuation and exits. People exit either to join or start a venture or to

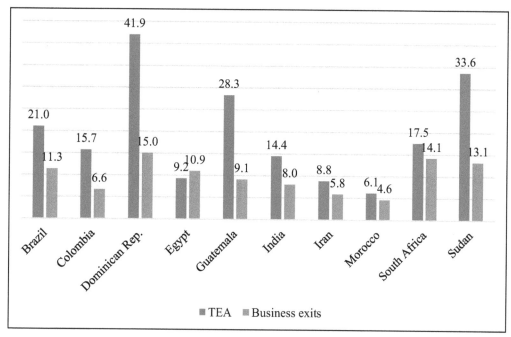

FIGURE 3.14   Business Exit and TEA: A Comparison of Low-Income Countries

**Source:** *GEM India Survey 2021–22*

discontinue a business. The most obvious, and usually most prevalent, relates to insufficient sales or profitability. In these turbulent times, the COVID pandemic was also a negative reason. But there are also positive reasons to discontinue a business, including the chance to sell the business at an advantageous price or some other business opportunity.

In India, TEA is as high as 14.4%, however, at the same time, the exit rate stands at 8%. This reflects that a greater number of entrepreneurs are trying to survive and exit is not the immediate decision taken by them. In Egypt, the rate of exit is higher than TEA. The highest rate of exit is found in the Dominican Republic at 15%. The lowest exit rate is in Morocco and it is also low in terms of total TEA (Figure 3.14).

## 3.18   Exit and Discontinuation Reasons Among the Low-Income Countries

This section has been analyzed for exit on the basis of three broad reasons, which fall under positive, negative but not including the COVID-19 impact, and finally explicitly due to COVID-19 impact. Figure 3.15 shows that the reasons for exit in India are due to negative reasons (4%), excluding the COVID-19 impact. This highlights that entrepreneurial activities could not have sustained because of sustainability factors or capital constraints or any other financial challenges faced by the respondents. And the second major reason is the COVID-19 impact, a lot of entrepreneurial activity came to halt in the nation due to lockdown and other restrictions in the last 2 years.

Sudan is a country that has been highly impacted on the entrepreneurial activity front owing to negative reasons for exit not including the COVID-19 impact. Brazil has been the most impacted nation among the ten countries that seem to have been impacted by COVID-19 the most.

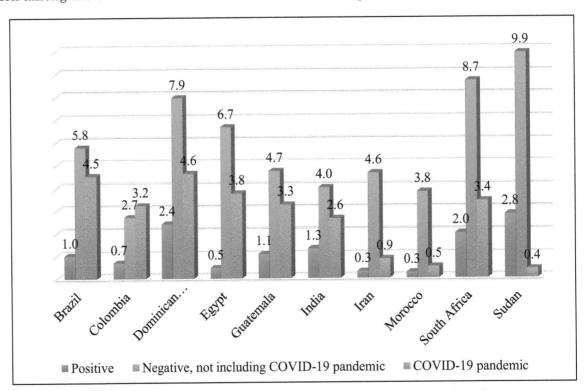

FIGURE 3.15   Reasons for Business Exit: A Comparison of Low-Income Countries

*Source: GEM India Survey 2021–22*

## 3.19    Motivation for Entrepreneurship

Individual motivation is a primary source of new businesses. In this latest 2021–22 data, survey questions for motivation are more clearly drafted and seek answers for what motivates people for entrepreneurship throughout the world. In India, motivations for business are majorly due to job scarcity, to continue family tradition, to build wealth, and so on. Motivation for entrepreneurial activity depends upon the resource access of an individual (Aldrich & Zimmer, 1986). Figure 3.16 depicts that global entrepreneurs want to make a difference in the world. It is highest in South Africa, 81.4% of the total TEA want to make a difference in the world and it is followed by India with 75.9% of the entrepreneurs who want to make a difference in the world.

Another important perspective in this series of outcomes is whether entrepreneurs build to make great wealth or high income out of their business. The data reveal that the highest 86.8% of entrepreneurs in Sudan seek entrepreneurship to build great wealth and increase income. This is followed by South Africa with 83.3% and further followed by India with 73.4% of Indian adults considering wealth creation as a major objective behind their entrepreneurial journey.

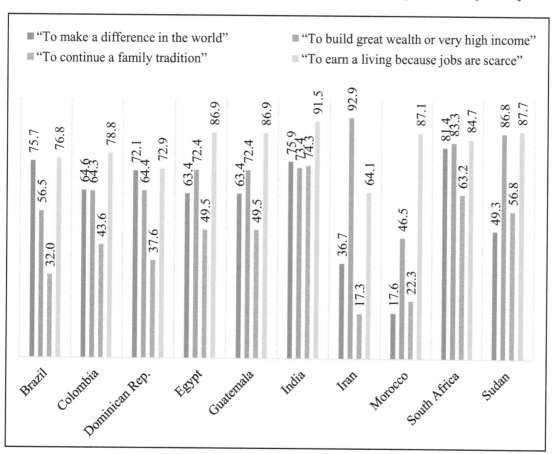

FIGURE 3.16    Entrepreneurial Motivation: A Comparison of Low-Income Countries in GEM

*Source: GEM India Survey 2021–22*

All these data points trigger an important understanding that low-income economies face high job scarcity and people want to be entrepreneurs because of that. It also leads to necessity-driven entrepreneurship in a country that is sometimes considered not much impactful. To make entrepreneurship more impactful in these countries, it is important to promote innovation-driven entrepreneurship and entrepreneurship for change. It will benefit these countries in the long term and help them achieve income, change in society, and greater prospects.

## 3.20  Growth Expectation

Growth is very important and helps us identify the prospects of a certain industry or enterprise. Growth is related to employment growth, innovation growth, sales growth, technological progress, and others. In GEM methodology, growth expectations are related to the percentage of the 18–64 population who expect to increase a particular number of employees in the next five years. The growth of jobs and work must encompass population growth that can lead to economic growth in the country. An increase in jobs in industry and enterprise has a direct relationship with the growth of the economy.

## 3.21  Employment Growth Expectation

New businesses that intend to employ more people are likely to have a greater impact than those expecting to employ their founder and no one else. Hence, this survey asks those starting or running a new business how many people they expect to employ in 5-year time. Therefore, in this section of results, the employment growth of the TEA is discussed. The data is a comparison of some participatory countries in a recent GEM survey. The pandemic has hit hard the employment expectation and it can be seen in this data as well. The majority of the surveyed individuals think that they will add 0 jobs to their business in the next few years and it is highest among the respondents from Dominican Republic (33.8%) and Sudan (20.4%). Around 6.7% of Indians and 7.1% of Brazilian respondents believe they will not add any new employees to their business. The job growth expectations of those starting or running a new business are set out in Figure 3.17.

The percentage of respondents who want to increase their employment by 1–5 jobs is also very low in Egypt, Morocco, Iran, and India. The percentage of TEA who want to increase their employment by more than six in the next few years is high in Guatemala, Columbia, and Brazil. The percentage has greatly been affected by the pandemic and it can be seen in the data point in Figure 3.17.

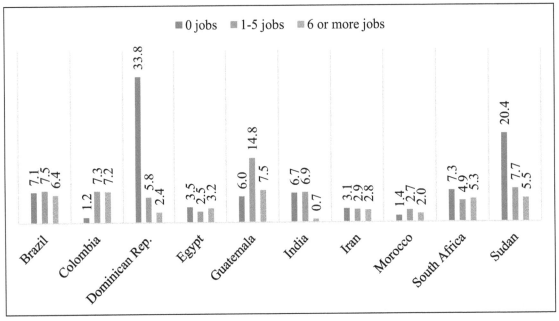

FIGURE 3.17   Growth Expectation of Job Creation in Low-Income Countries in GEM

*Source: GEM India Survey 2021–22*

## 3.22  Popular Sectors for Starting a Business

In this survey, the question is also asked to understand sector-wise business activities. The sector is classified into four broad sectors, that is, Extractive, including oil and gas, mining, and agriculture; Transforming, including manufacturing and transport; Business Services, including communications and professional services; and Consumer Services, including hotels and restaurants, retailing, and personal services.

The first two sectors (Extractive and Transformative) tend to have high importance in a small number of economies. Out of 10 low-income countries, the share of the Extractive sector in new start-ups exceeded one in five in just one economy (Sudan). In India, about 19% of existing entrepreneurs have reported that they are extractive sectors. The share of Transformative sector is largest in Egypt (39%) and then Iran (34%), and lowest in the Dominican Republic (13%). Services, with this share typically being much higher in high-income than in low-income economies. But only India, a Level C economy, has a lower share of new start-ups in Business Services (2%). Figure 3.18 indicates that the majority of business in low-income economies are in consumer-oriented services.

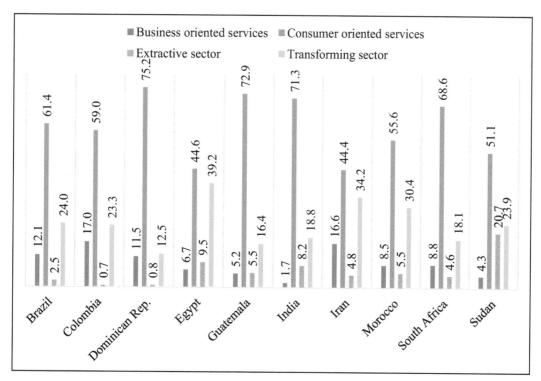

**FIGURE 3.18**  Sectors for Starting a Business

*Source: GEM India Survey 2021–22*

## 3.23  Impact of Pandemic on Business

In this section, an effort has been made to understand the impact of the pandemic and doing business in a low-income economy. By comparing rates in 2019 to those in 2020 and 2021, it can be seen that TEA and EBO rates have generally declined a little during the pandemic. Figure 3.19 indicates that the entrepreneurial response to the pandemic has been in a relatively high proportion of those starting or running new businesses. The portion of those starting or running a new business (TEA) and seeing pandemic-provided opportunities they wished to pursue was greater than those who are running established businesses (EBO). It is also evident that in India

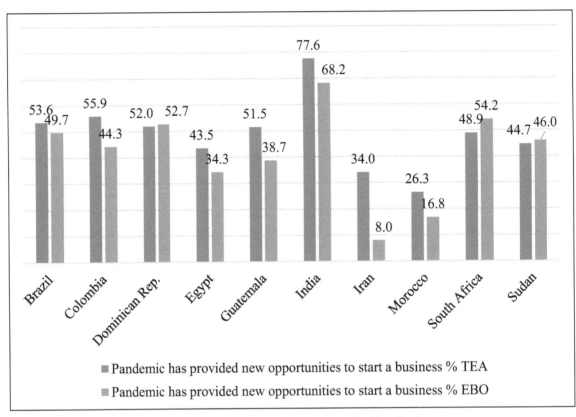

FIGURE 3.19    Pandemic as Opportunities for New Business

*Source:* *GEM India Survey 2021–22*

77.58% of new entrepreneurs reported that pandemic has provided them with new opportunities to start a business whereas, 68.23% of established business have given their consent for the same. It is important to mention here that for both parameters; India's rank is first among Level-C economies.

## 3.24    Pandemic as Problem

In this survey, respondents were also asked if starting or running a new business was more difficult than a year ago. The results are presented in Figure 3.20. In Level-C economies, the percentage of those who agreed that it was somewhat or much more difficult to start a business a year ago ranged from one in 4 (Egypt) to almost nine out of 10 (India and Iran). In general, this percentage is higher in the Level-C economies. More than half of those starting a business thought doing so was more difficult in nine out of 10 Level-C economies, six out of 18 Level-B and just three out of 19 Level-A economies (GEM Report 2021/2022).

## 3.25    Use of Digital Technology for Business

The pandemic has also impacted the process of business. For example, now much more business is conducted online, promoted through social media, paid for digitally, etc. To understand this impact, a question was also asked to the existing entrepreneurs whether they are going to use more digital technologies to sell their products or services in the next 6 months (Figure 3.21). In the Level-C economies that percentage ranged from 52% (South Africa) to 84% (Brazil).

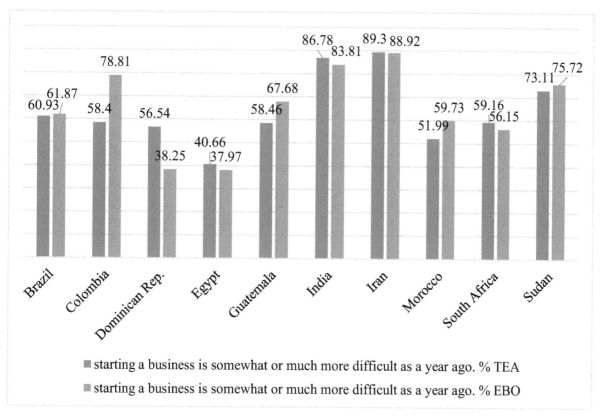

■ starting a business is somewhat or much more difficult as a year ago. % TEA
■ starting a business is somewhat or much more difficult as a year ago. % EBO

FIGURE 3.20    Pandemic as Problems for New Business

*Source:* GEM India Survey 2021/22

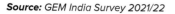

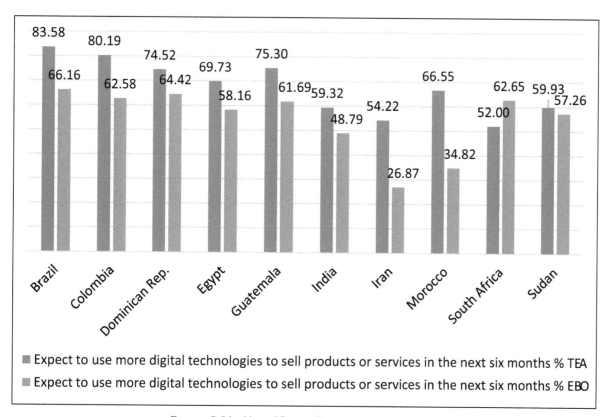

■ Expect to use more digital technologies to sell products or services in the next six months % TEA
■ Expect to use more digital technologies to sell products or services in the next six months % EBO

FIGURE 3.21    Use of Digital Technology for Business

*Source:* GEM India Survey 2021–22

## 3.26   Conclusion

The economies of the country have been hit hard by the COVID-19 pandemic. Since entrepreneurship is an engine of economic development, and one of the main sources of wealth creation and new jobs, the present report provides guidance to entrepreneurs on where to invest their resources and how to influence stakeholders for the kind of support they most need. Starting a business in any community depends upon perceptions of local business opportunities and the ease of starting a business, as well as an awareness of one's own capability and abilities. The present report clearly reflects that there is widespread awareness of entrepreneurship and some confidence in abilities. In India, youth perceives that they have high levels of awareness, opportunity recognition, perceived ease of starting a business, and self-confidence in having the skills and abilities to start the business. However, many intentions appear to be seriously constrained by the fear of failure.

However, it is also evident from the findings of low-income economies that many of those starting a new business considered that doing so was more difficult a year ago. Hence, on one hand, to promote entrepreneurship, removing those difficulties is the need of the hour in the low-income economies. On the other hand, many new entrepreneurs see new business opportunities as a result of the pandemic than those running established businesses. The results also indicate that in low-income economies more than one in two new entrepreneurs expect to increase the use of digital technologies to sell their products in the next six months. It indicates the preparedness of entrepreneurs for a changing business world.

It is important to mention here that the number of job-creation ambitions can be an important indicator of the economic impact potential of the new business. But the findings of low-income economies suggest that high levels of entrepreneurial activity may not easily translate into employment-intensive established businesses in the future.

# Entrepreneurial Framework Conditions in India: National Expert Survey (NES)

# 4

## 4.1 Overview

The entrepreneurial ecosystem is a set of social, economic, cultural, and political components, which is accumulatively built an environment for existing and potential entrepreneurs. A location's culture, size and density of its social networks, public laws, and economic structure impact the ease of accessing the resources available in the ecosystem for entrepreneurs (Spigel, 2020). Since the inception of the entrepreneurial ecosystem, Global Entrepreneurship Monitor (GEM) has concentrated on the factors that favor (or restrict) the development of new businesses. In light of this, GEM has suggested various measures to examine their impact on the entrepreneurship ecosystem, known as the framework conditions for entrepreneurship. These factors directly impact entrepreneurial prospects, entrepreneurial capacity, and entrepreneurial inclinations. Distinct areas and economies have different entrepreneurial framework conditions, so it is essential to analyze them in light of the local environment. We have 11 key dimensions that define the entrepreneurial Framework. Figure 4.1 unfold these dimensions.

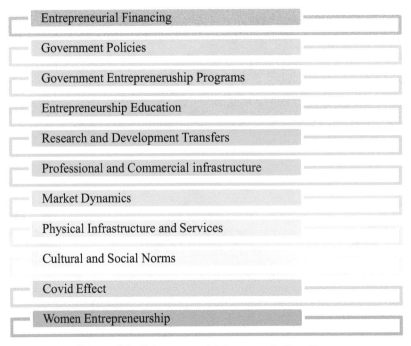

Entrepreneurial Financing

Government Policies

Government Entrepreneruship Programs

Entrepreneurship Education

Research and Development Transfers

Professional and Commercial infrastructure

Market Dynamics

Physical Infrastructure and Services

Cultural and Social Norms

Covid Effect

Women Entrepreneurship

FIGURE 4.1   Entrepreneurial Framework Conditions

*Source: GEM India Survey 2021–22*

## 4.2   Entrepreneurial Framework Conditions in India

Entrepreneurial framework conditions include various factors that help to measure the condition of the entrepreneurial ecosystem. The Indian entrepreneurial framework conditions are split into different classifications for a thorough examination. This creates a comprehensive list of 18 factors, namely; (1) sufficiency of financing for entrepreneurs, (2) easiness to get financing for entrepreneurs, (3) government concrete policies: priority and support, (4) government policies: bureaucracy and taxes, (5) government programs, (6) entrepreneurial level of education at primary and secondary, (7) entrepreneurial level of education at vocational, professional, college, and university, (8) research and development transference, (9) professional and commercial infrastructure access, (10) internal market dynamics, (11) internal market burdens, (12) general

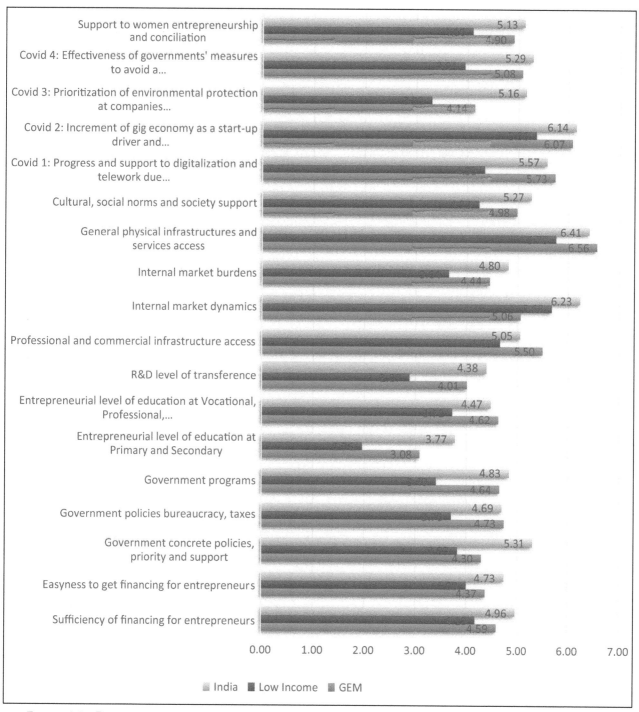

**FIGURE 4.2** Entrepreneurial Framework Conditions of India and Comparison with Low-Income and GEM Countries

*Source: GEM India Survey 2021–22*

physical infrastructures and services access, (13) cultural, social norms, and society support, (14) COVID 1: progress and support to digitalization and telework due to the pandemic, (15) COVID 2: increment of gig economy as a start-up driver and business model due to the pandemic, (16) COVID 3: prioritization of environmental protection at companies, (17) governments' impulse of the green agenda due to the pandemic, and (18) COVID 4: effectiveness of governments' measures to avoid a significant decline in new businesses and controlling health-harming economy as little as possible and support to women entrepreneurship and conciliation.

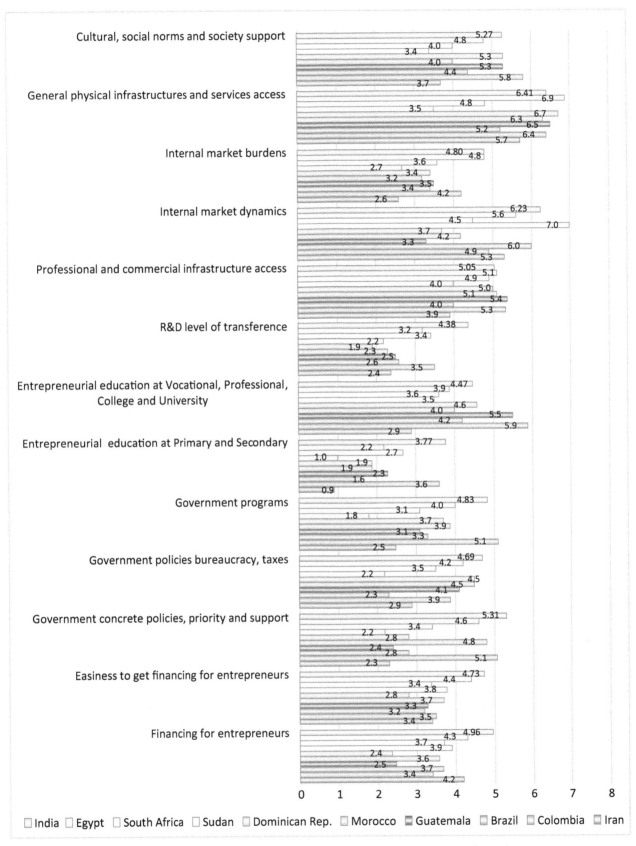

**FIGURE 4.3**   Entrepreneurial Framework Conditions of Low-Income Countries

**Source:** *GEM India Survey 2021–22*

India's condition is better in all the factors compared to other GEM countries, especially low-income countries. India has performed competently in government concrete policies, priority and support, and support to women entrepreneurship and conciliation. Except for the impact of the global pandemic, the country is adding across pillars an enhanced entrepreneurial ecosystem. General physical infrastructure and services access and internal market dynamics are the most progressive conditions in India, followed by the increment of the gig economy as a start-up driver and business model due to the pandemic.

## 4.3 Entrepreneurship Framework Conditions: Comparison of Low-Income Countries

The entrepreneurial framework conditions of 10 low-income nations, including India, Iran, Colombia, Brazil, Guatemala, Morocco, the Dominican Republic, Sudan, South Africa, and Egypt, have been examined as part of the GEM India 2020–21 survey. We can compare the ecosystems of low-income economies with the help of this analysis. It would provide a clearer picture of where the Indian ecosystem stands compared to other developing nations.

Among these low-income economies, with NECI 5.0 and a ranking of 16T, India has been tremendously good as an entrepreneurial ecosystem. India is a leading ecosystem for entrepreneurs as compared to the other low-income economies, especially in financing entrepreneurs, easiness to getting financing for entrepreneurs, and government concrete policies, priority and support. All these economies are very focused on access to the general physical infrastructures and services. One least developed factor is entrepreneurial education in primary and secondary schools. India and Colombia have made strenuous efforts to entrepreneurship education in schools compared to other economies. India has been significantly different from other low-income economies in the context of research and development transfers. India is investing in research and development and government programs to enhance its entrepreneurial ecosystem holistically. Colombia is performing impressively in entrepreneurial education at vocational, professional, college, and university levels, and Sudan's condition of internal market dynamics are very influential among other countries.

## 4.4 Entrepreneurship Financing in India

### 4.4.1 Financial Environment

Entrepreneurship financing as a framework condition concentrates on the availability of financial resources for entrepreneurs, both equity and debt. This includes all grants and subsidies. In India, the financial ecosystem for entrepreneurs is highly favorable. Every year, the country puts many resources to firmly back the financial ecosystem of the country. This parameter has eight further dimensions, which try to analyze equity funding, debt funding, government subsidies, funding from informal investors including friends and family, professional business angels funding, venture capitalists funding, initial public offerings, and micro-funding, which includes popular options like crowdfunding. Amongst all these parameters, debt funding is the most vigorous dimension, followed by government subsidies and informal investors. The financial ecosystem has become weaker in each circumstance analogous to last year. The government initiatives are not being implemented significantly compared to the prior year, causing all other financial metrics to decrease, with debt funding showing the most negligible impact.

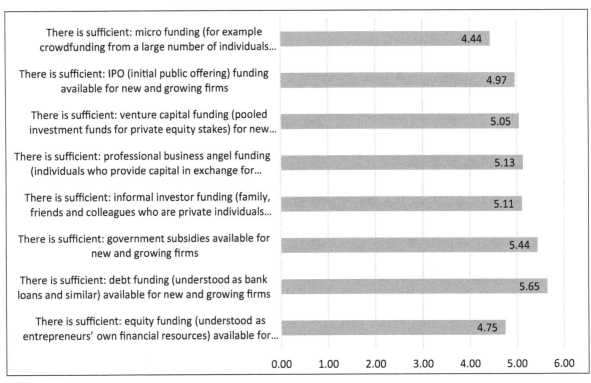

**FIGURE 4.4**    Financial Environment Related to Entrepreneurship in India

*Source: GEM India Survey 2021–22*

## 4.4.2   Easiness to Get Financing for Entrepreneurs

Finance is the most crucial part of the entrepreneurship ecosystem, but easy access to finance for entrepreneurs is also essential. The government and other institutions are supporting

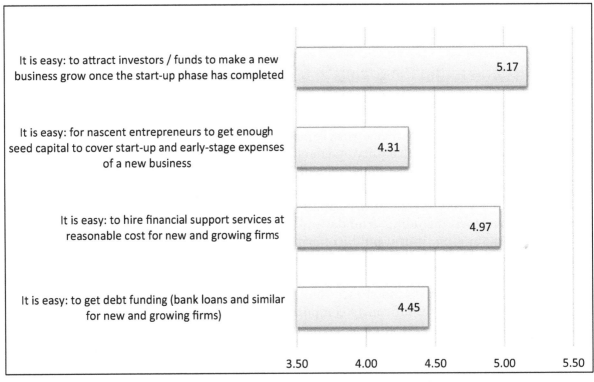

**FIGURE 4.5**    Easiness to Get Financing for Entrepreneurs in India

*Source: GEM India Survey 2021–22*

start-ups to grow. Entrepreneurs want to access financial services at a reasonable cost. It is difficult for nascent and existing entrepreneurs to get enough seed capital for a new business to cover start-up and early-stage expenses. Getting borrowing from banks and other sources is not easy; however, it gets more difficult for new and growing firms.

## 4.5   Government Concrete Policies, Priorities, and Support in India

Government policies emphasize the support that entrepreneurs get through public policies. It tries to understand up to what extent these policies are supporting the enterprises. The parameter is further divided into three dimensions. The support for new and growing firms at the national level has grown significantly compared to the local level.

Compared to the last year, all dimensions show a fall in government support and policies. The score in this area has fallen by significant margin points. Local governments must take significant steps to facilitate a favorable ecosystem for entrepreneurs. The local government should emphasize improving the support system to provide better conditions to entrepreneurs.

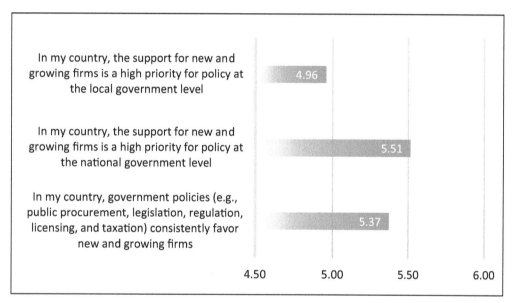

FIGURE 4.6   Government Support and Policies in India

*Source:* GEM India Survey 2021–22

## 4.6   Government Policies, Taxes, and Bureaucracy in India

Taxes and bureaucracy are the second component of government policy as a whole. This aspect takes care of taxes and regulations that would support the new and growing firms. The parameter has five dimensions through which it is evaluated. According to the analysis of the GEM experts, entrepreneurs can register for new businesses at a reasonable cost with the help of government policies. Though, compared to the previous year, the time required for registration has increased, which needs to be improved for a smooth business establishment. As per experts, there is a scope to change the mentality about taxes and government regulation by making entrepreneur-friendly policies.

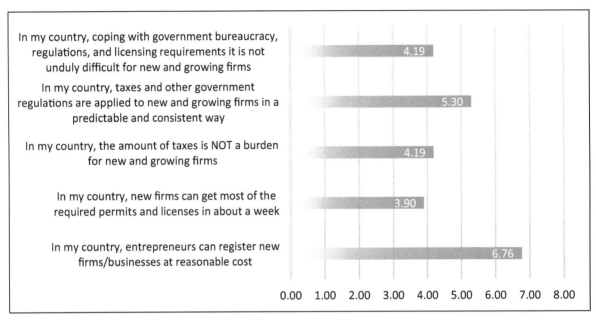

**FIGURE 4.7**   Taxes and Bureaucracy in India

*Source: GEM India Survey 2021–22*

## 4.7   Government Programs in India

The government organizes various entrepreneurship programs both at the federal and local levels. These programs help potential and existing enterprises in expansion through the intervention of competency and skill-building initiatives. According to the experts' survey, an adequate number of government programs effectively support new and growing firms. In the 2020–21 survey, science parks and incubators effectively supported new and growing firms. However, in 2021–22 it decreased by 1.45 points, which should be improved in the upcoming years. There is further scope for improvement in programs for better accessibility for new and growing firms.

## 4.8   Education—Primary and Secondary

Entrepreneurship education aims to encourage and stimulate the creation of new firms and grow the existing ones by raising students' awareness about entrepreneurship. This segment is divided into two categories; one is focused on education at the basic school level (primary and secondary), and the other is focused on the post-secondary level (higher education such as vocational centers, colleges, and business schools).

Primary school-level entrepreneurship education in India is represented by Figure 4.9. Various initiatives are required to improve the existing structure of entrepreneurship education. Though, India has worked better as compared to low-income-group countries. Three parameters have been used to explain education at the secondary level. While evaluating primary and secondary education, experts explain that education enhances students' creativity, self-sufficiency, and personal initiative. It is alarming for India as entrepreneurial education at the primary and secondary levels has significantly decreased from the previous year. All three areas need to be improved, and targeted actions should be taken to alter the learning environment.

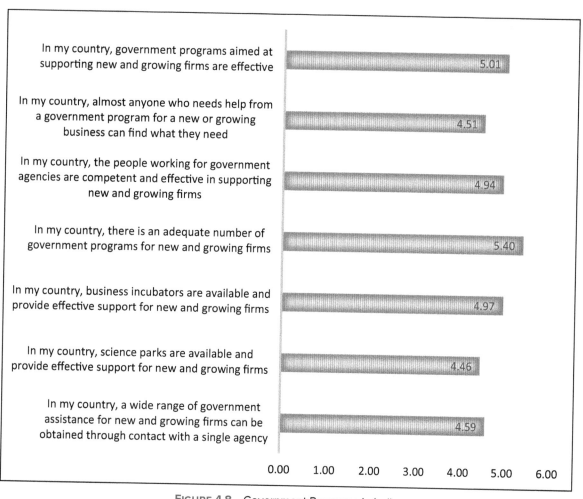

FIGURE 4.8   Government Programs in India

*Source: GEM India Survey 2021–22*

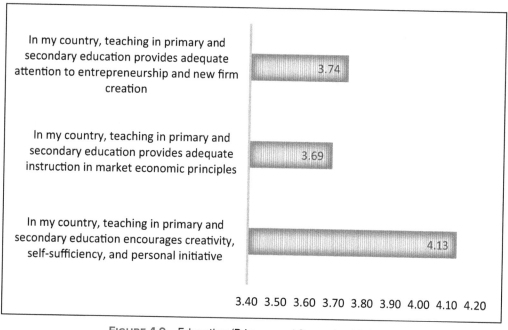

FIGURE 4.9   Education (Primary and Secondary) in India

*Source: GEM India Survey 2021–22*

## 4.9    Education—Post-Secondary Level in India

The second category of entrepreneurial education, which deals with post-secondary level education, is represented in Figure 4.10. In India, post-secondary education is slightly better than primary and intermediate education. The vocational, professional, and continuing education systems provide adequate preparation for starting and growing new firms. However, all three aspects have shrunk from the previous year. India stands third in performance compared to other low-income countries, highlighting the need for considerable improvement.

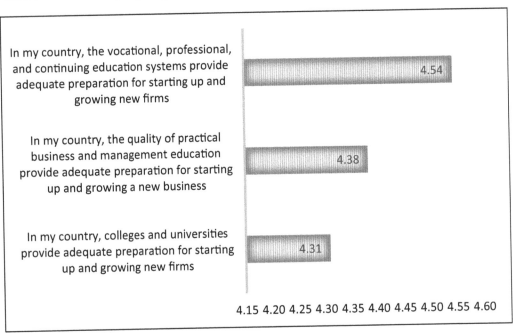

FIGURE 4.10    Education (Post-secondary level) in India

*Source:* GEM India Survey 2021–22

## 4.10    Research and Development in India

Research and development support innovation and the societal problem-solving process. For the sake of financial gain and business expansion, the solutions are commercialized. The expert used six parameters to analyze this area. There is significant support from the science and technology base for creating world-class new technology-based ventures, at least in one area. We can analyze the positive role of government subsidies for new and growing firms to acquire new technologies. All of the parameters indicate a usual decline from the prior year.

## 4.11    Professional and Commercial Infrastructure Access in India

The availability of professional and commercial services and the resources that support new and growing businesses are the key objectives of professional and commercial infrastructure. In this regard, India has been performing incredibly well. Experts analyze six different aspects for an overall assessment. India has a favorable ecosystem in all areas, but access to good contractors, suppliers, and availability of contractors at a reasonable cost needs to be improved. The most favorable aspect available to new and growing firms is access to cloud computing services at

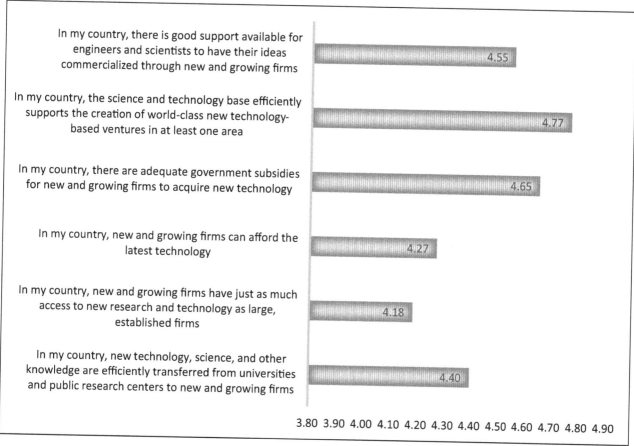

FIGURE 4.11   Research and Development in India

**Source:** *GEM India Survey 2021–22*

affordable prices and good banking services (checking/transaction accounts, foreign exchange transactions, letters of credit). India can create a more favorable ecosystem with further improvements to its infrastructure.

## 4.12   Internal Market Dynamics in India

The dynamics of the market comprise several elements that influence the firm. The entrance rules have been divided into two sections by GEM experts. Market dynamics are represented in Figure 4.13.

Experts examine the degree of change in the market using market dynamics. Business-to-business dynamics and market dynamics for consumer goods and services are two other dynamics that are examined. Compared to last year, both parameters have decreased. India has a robust ecosystem in the context of internal market dynamics, which is one of the framework conditions.

## 4.13   Internal Market Burdens

The second aspect of entry regulation is the market burden, which investigates the ease for new enterprises to enter new and established markets. In order to investigate this parameter for studies, four components are considered, as shown in Figure 4.14. Overall, the business

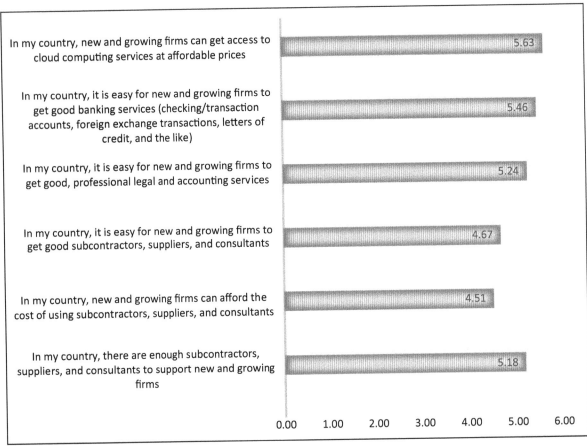

**FIGURE 4.12**    Professional and Commercial Infrastructure Access in India

*Source:* *GEM India Survey 2021–22*

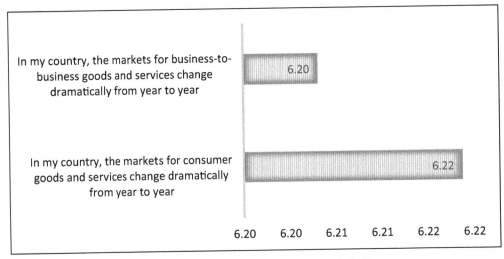

**FIGURE 4.13**    Internal Market Dynamics in India

*Source:* *GEM India Survey*

environment is usual and straightforward for emerging and new companies to enter the market. The ecosystem is average in terms of law and how well-existing businesses are performing. India is also doing a fantastic job in combating the unfair restrictions put in place by legacy businesses.

As compared to last year's scoring, internal market burdens have declined. We can observe many shifts across different factors. The most performing factor is an easy entry into the new market. It is a crucial factor that would ease the entry of new and young entrepreneurs. One factor

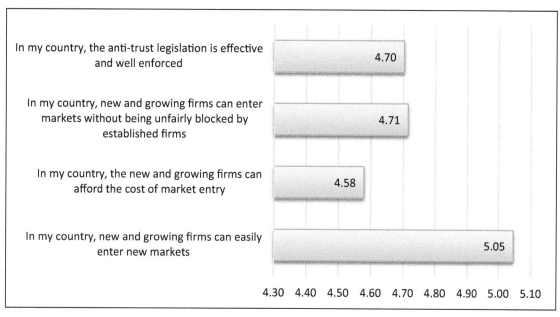

FIGURE 4.14    Internal Market Burden in India

*Source: GEM India Survey 2021–22*

that needs attention is the effective and well-enforced anti-trust legislation. This factor scores less compared to other factors of internal market openness and has also slipped by some points compared to last year.

## 4.14   Physical Infrastructure in India

Physical infrastructure works like a booster to the business and helps in providing services more efficiently and comfortably. Under this framework condition, experts study how easily entrepreneurs can access physical resources. Affordable spaces, access, and affordable utilities like gas, water, electricity, and communication are part of this framework condition. Figure 4.15 displays seven factors with their points for this year. India is performing well in all the factors, and there is a little decline compared to the previous year.

There are significant scores in all the factors except the physical infrastructure support for new and growing firms, which needs to be improved. The access to communication in about a week and the affordable cost of essential utilities are the most significant factor in this area.

## 4.15   Cultural, Social Norms, and Society Support in India

This condition takes care of the social and cultural norms that encourage new business methods and activities that would help in increasing personal wealth and income. The analysis is done through five different factors. Altogether, this framework condition contributes to making the ecosystem favorable for entrepreneurs. The most positive aspect is that the country's national culture emphasizes the responsibility toward the individual in managing their own life. There has been an equal decline in the expert scores across various factors compared to last year's scores. There is a massive decline in risk-taking encouraged by national culture, which means post-covid situation has inclined society toward sensitivity in taking risks. The fall in encouragement to creativity and innovativeness is also needed to enhance. Necessary actions should be taken to switch the current scenario and improve the environment for entrepreneurs.

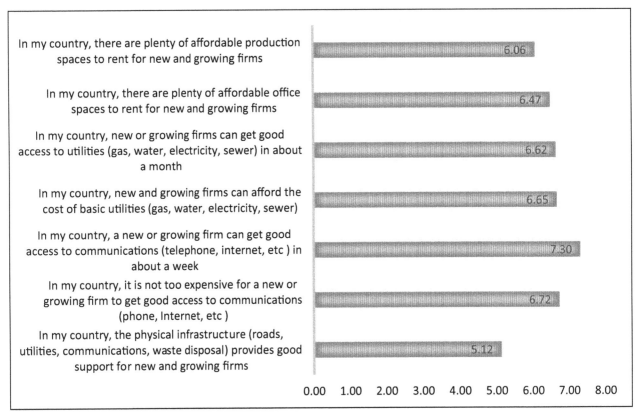

**FIGURE 4.15**   Physical Infrastructure in India

*Source: GEM India Survey 2021–22*

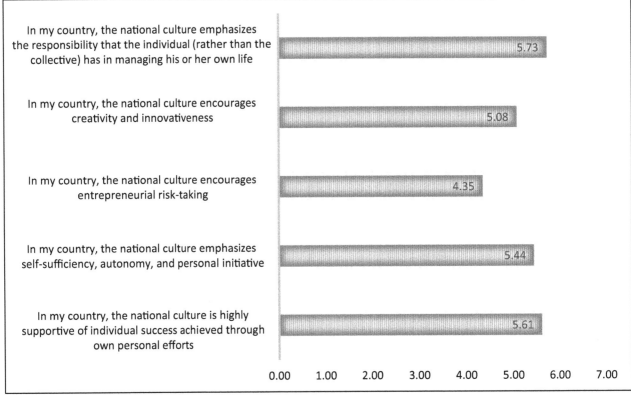

**FIGURE 4.16**   Social and Cultural Norms in India

*Source: GEM India Survey*

## 4.16   Covid Effect

The year 2020–21 has been challenging for economies across the world. Every sector had to suffer market disruptions as a result of the pandemic. However, nations have tried to control the situation by providing various supports. The government has played the most critical role in assisting multiple industries contributing to the economy's recovery. This segment is divided into four categories. First, the progress and support for digitalization and telework due to the pandemic. Second is the increment of the gig economy as a start-up driver and business model due to the pandemic. The third is the prioritization of environmental protection at companies' and governments' impulse of the green agenda due to the pandemic. Last is the effectiveness of government's measures to avoid a significant decline in new businesses and control the health-harming economy as little as possible. The Government of India took adequate steps to support the entrepreneurs. This government support helped the firms to survive and handle their losses.

### 4.16.1   Progress and Support for Digitalization and Telework due to the Pandemic

The first category under covid effect includes three parameters based on which experts have analyzed the impact of digitalization and telework. There is a significant number of firms that have promoted work from home as a result of the COVID-19 pandemic. New and growing firms prefer to spend money on digitalization to become more competitive. Experts find that government support like subsidies, tax benefits, or training is less significant and needs to be enhanced in upcoming years.

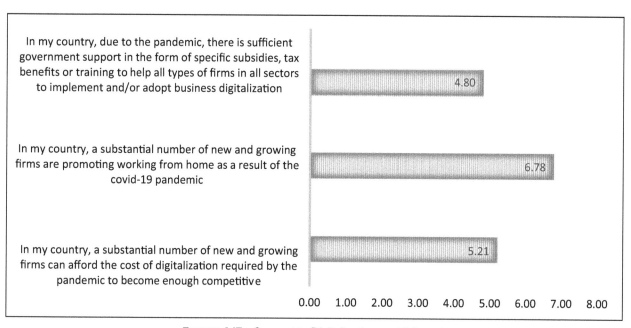

FIGURE 4.17   Support to Digitalization and Telework

*Source: GEM India Survey 2021–22*

### 4.16.2   Increment of the Gig Economy as a Start-up Driver and Business Model due to the Pandemic

Figure 4.18 represents an assessment of the gig economy, a type of labor market characterized by the prevalence of short-term contracts or freelance work as opposed to permanent jobs and a gig-based business model. Experts find significant effects of the pandemic on both parts.

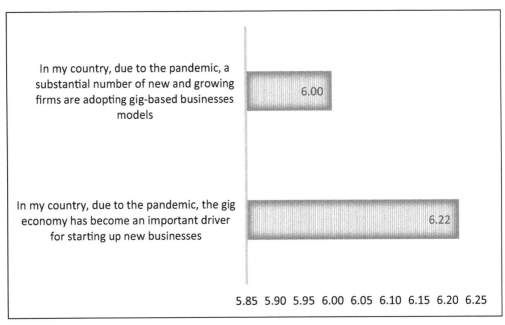

**FIGURE 4.18**    Gig Economy and Gig-Based Business Model

*Source: GEM India Survey 2021–22*

### 4.16.3    Prioritization of Environmental Protection at Companies and Governments' Impulse of the Green Agenda due to the Pandemic

The pandemic has pushed the government and companies to think about environmental issues. Figure 4.19 explains two parameters, including the government's focus on taking effective measures to promote sustainability and environmental awareness among all firms with a specific environmental policy, which has a good impact, as per the experts. Still, the second parameter about the prioritization of the environment by firms above profit is low, which needs to be improved in the future. More awareness is required by both the sides of government and firms to protect and promote sustainability.

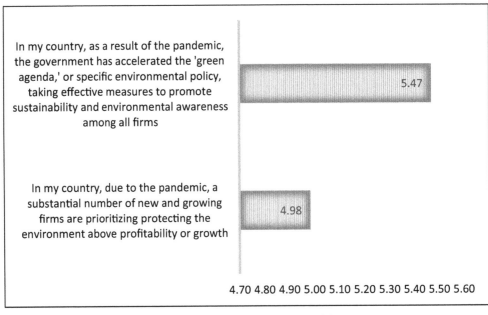

**FIGURE 4.19**    Environment Protection and Awareness

*Source: GEM India Survey 202122*

## 4.17 Effectiveness of Government's Measures to Control Health Crisis and Avoid Significant Decline of New Businesses

This category explains the decisions and measures taken by the government to deal with the health crisis. The government's decision has helped people while fighting a global pandemic, and they have tried to protect the economy. While the measures adopted by the government during the first 12 months of the pandemic to avoid a decline in the number of firms and the associated job were inappropriate, more effective steps were required from the government's side. Considering the global situation, the performance was satisfactory, as per the experts.

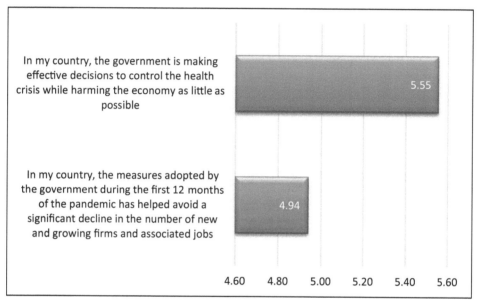

FIGURE 4.20   Government Decisions and Measures to Control the Effect of Pandemic

*Source: GEM India Survey 2021–22*

## 4.18 Support for Women Entrepreneurship and Conciliation in India

The increasing presence of women as entrepreneurs has led to significant business and economic growth in the country. Women-owned business enterprises play a prominent role in society by generating employment opportunities in the country, bringing in demographic shifts, and inspiring the next generation of women founders. Figure 4.21 explains the six parameters on which experts have given their scores. Teleworking has impacted most positively and improved the work–life balance of women. Now female entrepreneurs are getting access to finance and public procurement easily compared to men; this shows the availability of equal opportunity to men and women in India. But encouragement to women in the national culture to become an entrepreneur and sufficient support services (i.e., child-care and home service) is not prevalent in our country. That shows a strict need to improve these parameters to create a suitable environment for female entrepreneurs to establish themselves and grow. As per the experts, there is a need to make a more favorable ecosystem for women to become entrepreneurs.

## 4.19 Government Action and Affect: Positive and Negative

The world has been adjusting to the repercussions of the virus almost two years after the World Health Organization declared COVID-19 a pandemic. The pandemic's toll on the whole healthcare

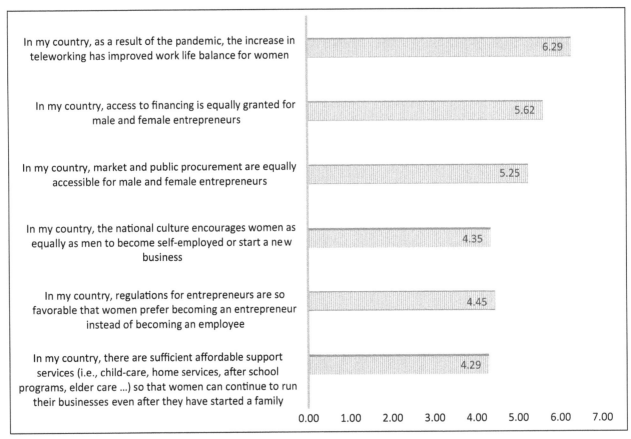

**FIGURE 4.21**   Support to Women Entrepreneurship and Conciliation

*Source: GEM India Survey 2021–22*

system has had the most significant effects, followed by the economic toll, which has been more enduring and pervasive. The country's ecosystem and development have been significantly impacted by lockdown and COVID protocols. Financial support, general government actions, government initiatives, and government health and welfare initiatives all harm the environment. The impact of financial services was very positive after government subsidies, employment preservation and wages, credit moratorium, deferment of tax liabilities, and loan extensions. The firms have received the benefit of financial support and government steps to control the negative effect on the economy. Government action has positively affected policies, the digitalization of companies, and government programs.

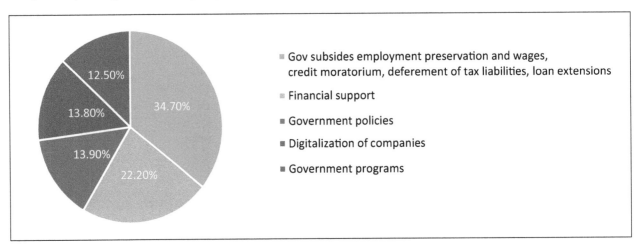

**FIGURE 4.22**   Positive Impact on Entrepreneurship Ecosystem

*Source: GEM India Survey 2021–22 (recommendations in percentages)*

Figure 4.23 explains the adverse effect of government actions on the ecosystem. A negative effect can be found due to lockdown, restrictions, and covid protocols, which shut down various economic activities. Loan extensions, deferment of tax liabilities, and government subsidies have also negatively affected the entrepreneurship ecosystem of India.

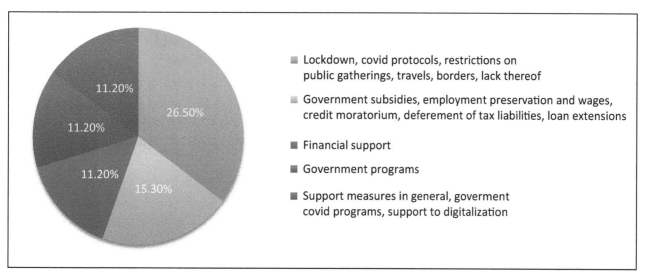

**FIGURE 4.23** Negative Impact on Entrepreneurship Ecosystem

*Source: GEM India Survey 21–22, (recommendations in percentages)*

## 4.20 Fostering Factors and Recommendations to Strengthen Entrepreneurship in India

Figure 4.24 shows the fostering factors for entrepreneurial activities in India. The experts have found that access to physical infrastructure and different performances of a small, medium, and large companies are the main fostering factors in India. These findings support the evidence that various entrepreneurship education, research and development transfers, and market openness are equally essential. Moreover, multiple institutions are working to strengthen entrepreneurship education, and private institutions are also shifting their interest toward developing an

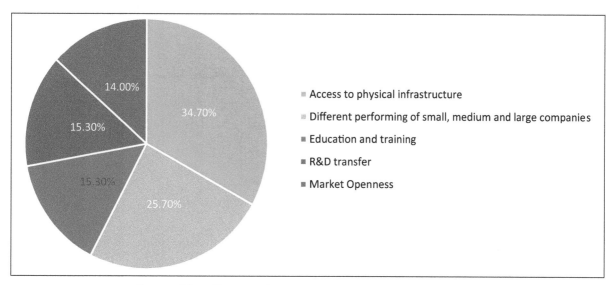

**FIGURE 4.24** Fostering Factors for Entrepreneurial Activity in India

*Source: GEM India Survey 2021–22 (fostering factors in percentages)*

entrepreneurship culture in their environment. The Government of India has taken different steps to promote research and development to foster innovative solutions for society. There are more opportunities for companies to invest, and a single-window redressal system has been promoted to address the smooth flow of investment in the country by the Government of India.

The experts' primary recommendation is to improve financial support for the novice and existing entrepreneurs so they can easily start and grow their businesses. Education and training play an essential role in building the entrepreneurship ecosystem. The government should focus on creating sound learning opportunities and developing human resource infrastructure for the growth of young entrepreneurs. The experts also recommend in Figure 4.25 that government programs and cultural and social norms should be improved and developed in a structured form to construct more advantageous circumstances to create and expand the enterprise.

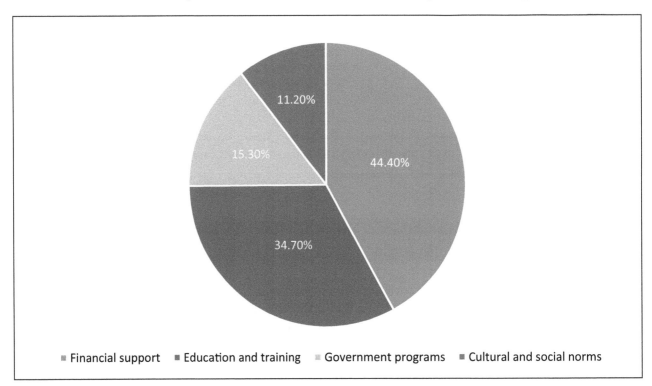

FIGURE 4.25    Recommendations to Improve Entrepreneurial Activity in India

*Source: GEM India Survey 2020–21, (recommendations in percentages)*

# Entrepreneurial Activities and Entrepreneurship Ecosystems In India

**5**

## 5.1  Introduction

Global Entrepreneurship Monitor (GEM) research is a country-wide survey of entrepreneurs, adults, nascent entrepreneurs, established entrepreneurs, female entrepreneurs, experts, and start-up founders to understand the status of the entrepreneurship and perceptions of the youth about the economies. The GEM research is acknowledged worldwide as one of the primary data-based research for entrepreneurship throughout the world. GEM has retained an important position with reference to researchers and policymakers to enhance the global outlook of entrepreneurship in an economy. The GEM data includes personal perspectives to entrepreneurship, societal perspectives to entrepreneurship as well as expert views on the ecosystem to analyze and look into the entrepreneurship status of the country.

The GEM India has been publishing the GEM India report since 2013. The GEM India report is a source of great information for entrepreneurial motivations, perception, and activities of the country. The reports analysis provides a range of new information relevant to the entrepreneurship ecosystem as well. The growth of entrepreneurship in the country is clearly visible. A significant improvement can be seen in the last 5 years on almost all key indicators of entrepreneurial activities and ecosystem in the countries. In this chapter, an effort is made to understand the trend of entrepreneurship activities and its related dimension in India.

## 5.2  Trends of Individual Attributes in India

In this section, an attempt has been made to understand the growth of individual attributes of the country in last 5 years. As discussed in Chapter 3, the individual attributes have been defined in terms of Perceived Opportunity, Perceived Capability, Fear of Failing Perception of Easiness to Start a Business, and Entrepreneurial Intentions. Figure 5.1 indicates that there is a significant growth for all five indicators of individual attributes. It implies that youth of the country has now perceived that they have better opportunities and they are more capable with well-defined intention to start the business. They are also thinking that starting a new business is easier than a few years back. It is very clear that the perception of our youth for all attributes is much higher in 2021–22 than 2017–18.

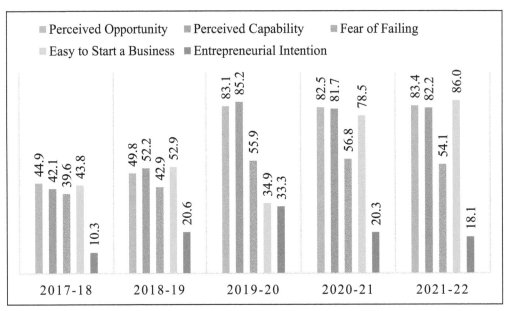

FIGURE 5.1   Trends of Individual Attributes in India

*Source:* GEM India Survey 2021–22

## 5.3    Total Entrepreneurial Activities in India

The result presented in Figure 5.2 reveals that total entrepreneurship activities rate in India has increased from 9.3% in 2017–18 to 14.4% in 2021–22. It is an important mention here that total entrepreneurial activity (TEA) includes Nascent Entrepreneurship and New Business Ownership. Along with TEA both have increased significantly in the same period of time. The increase in Nascent Entrepreneurship is 4.9% in 2017–18 to 7.2% in 2021–22. Similarly, in the case of New Business Ownership it is from 4.4% to 7.1% for the same period of time. On the similar line, the established entrepreneurship rate has also increased from 6.2% to 8.5% from 2017–18 to 2021–22. However, the established business rate was higher (11.9%) in 2019–2020.

It is also evident that COVID-19 pandemic has a significant impact on Entrepreneurship Activities and its related dimensions. It can be observed in Figure 5.2 that there is a significant decline in almost all dimensions of entrepreneurship activity in the year of 2020–2021.

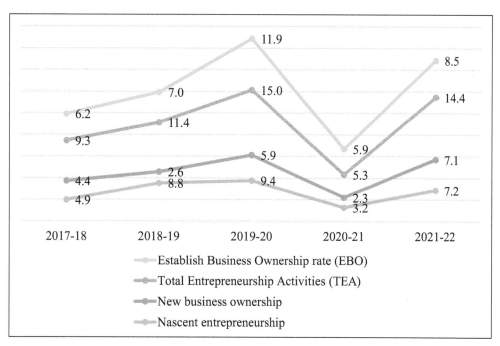

FIGURE 5.2    Total Entrepreneurship Activities in India in Last 5 Years

*Source: GEM India Survey 2021–22*

## 5.4    Entrepreneurial Finance and Government Policy for Entrepreneurship

The National Expert Survey (NES) provides us a holistic understanding about country's ecosystem for entrepreneurship development. In this survey, information was gathered from experts in the field of entrepreneurship, start-ups, policymaking, financial institutions and academics. As discussed in Chapter 2, the GEM has identified nine Entrepreneurship Framework Conditions (EFCs) to assess ecosystem for entrepreneurship in any country. For better understanding, we have categorized all nine EFCSs into three categories. The first category includes entrepreneurial finance and government policy and support, the second category contains market dynamics and infrastructures and the third category includes education and culture and social norms.

Figure 5.3 explains trends growth in the availability of finance, support, and relevance of government policy and government entrepreneurship programs. It is evident from the findings that expert's rating has increased in the last 5 years. It is important to mention here that finance and other government support has been highlighted by a number of researchers as an important factor for the business start-up and growth in India. Experts also consider government policy framing and implementation as another important aspect for the development of entrepreneurship in the country. However, the rating of all four EFCs is the highest in the financial year 2020–21. It indicates that after lockdown government has taken extra efforts for developing and strengthening entrepreneurship in the country.

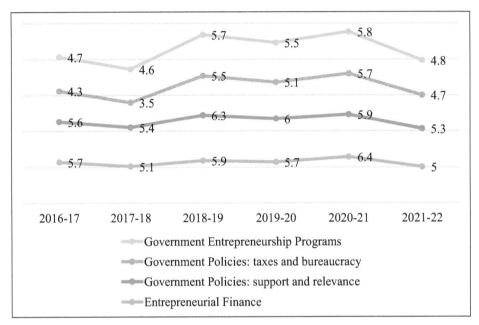

**FIGURE 5.3**    Entrepreneurial Finance and Government Policy for Entrepreneurship

*Source: GEM India Survey 2021–22*

## 5.5   Market Dynamics, R&D, and Infrastructure in India

In this section, an attempt has been made to understand the status of market dynamics, commercial infrastructures, R&D facilities, and basic infrastructure in the country. GEM has defined the market dynamic in terms of internal market openness and has two parts: internal market burdens and entry regulation. The data presented in Figure 5.4 indicate that the rating of experts gradually increase in favor of entrepreneurship. Experts of the country also rated the access of commercial and legal infrastructure favorably. The rating of Research and Development (R&D) facilities got good attention of experts and it has been increasing during the last 5 years. The rating of physical infrastructure is highest among all the five EFCs. It indicates the physical infrastructure for entrepreneurship is favorable in the country. The highest rating in financial year 2020–21 reveals government additional support within and after COVID-19.

## 5.6   Education and Cultural and Social Norms for Entrepreneurship in India

Figure 5.5 explains the status of education and cultural and social norms for entrepreneurship in India. GEM has categorized the education into two categories: (1) Entrepreneurial Education at School Level and (2) Entrepreneurial Education at Post-School Stage. It can be seen in the figure that entrepreneurial education at school level has witnessed no significant growth over the 5 years whereas education at post-school stage got little better rating by the experts. It implies that India needs special focus and approach to improve entrepreneurial education in the country. It is very clear from the results that culture and social norms are very supportive for

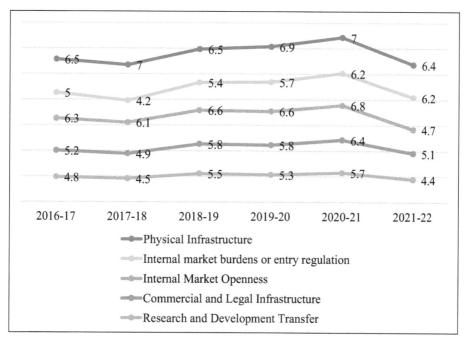

**FIGURE 5.4** Market Dynamics, R&D and Infrastructure in the Last 5 Years

*Source: GEM India Survey 2021–22*

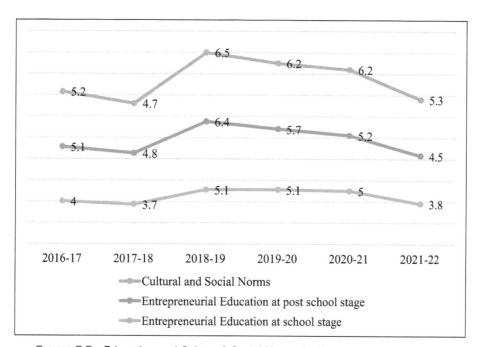

**FIGURE 5.5** Education and Culture & Social Norms for Entrepreneurship in India

*Source: GEM India Survey 2021–22*

entrepreneurship and also increasing day by day. The impact of lockdown can be seen in terms of decrease in ratings for financial years 2020–21 and 2021–22.

## 5.7  Conclusion and Policy Implication

The population of youth of the country is a deciding factor for the development of entrepreneurship in the future of the country. Currently, Government of India has been promoting entrepreneurship with utmost enthusiasm and policymakers hope that entrepreneurship is the key for economic development of the country. The number of start-ups, unicorns has been increasing and adding to the list. The easiest way to set a thing into the minds is done through its youths. The change in the mindset and positive thoughts for entrepreneurship will lead to a greater entrepreneurial activity in the country. A culture of entrepreneurship will boost the entrepreneurship automatically.

Entrepreneurship education at both secondary- and higher-level needs immediate attention of government as well as policymakers. Though many of the education boards and institutions have included entrepreneurship in the curriculum but its implementation is still not satisfactory. Only introducing the education is not sufficient but educational institutions need to recruit trained manpower to implement entrepreneurship education successfully. Hence, it is important to open the way to school boards and higher-education institutions to introduce entrepreneurship as a part of their curriculum to foster entrepreneurship in the country.

The NES data reveal that the EFCs are growing but experts have some reservations for some of the framework conditions. Though, experts have opined that government policy and subsidies, employment preservation and wages, credit moratorium, deferment of tax liabilities, loan extensions, and digitalization of companies have very positive impact on entrepreneurship. However, lockdown, COVID protocols, restrictions on public gatherings, travels, borders, have negative impact on entrepreneurship. The finding of this research also indicates that to promote the entrepreneurship in the country, policymakers need to facilitate financial supports, and government programs need to be provided to potential and existing entrepreneurs.

## 5.8   Key Points from the Adult Population Survey (APS)

- There is a strong percentage of respondents who positively answered the "know someone who has started a new business". The data highlights that around 63% of the population know someone who has started a business recently or lately.

- The data for percentage of population who perceive that there are good opportunities in their area for new business has gained positivity from the preceding years. The data shows that 83.4% of the population perceives that there is a good opportunity to start a business in their area. Of the 47 economies who participated, India has ranked second for perceived opportunities.

- About 86% of youth perceived that they have sufficient skills and knowledge to start a business. Out of the 47 economies who participated, India has ranked fourth for perceived opportunities.

- About 54% of youth have reported that they are not able to start the business due to the fear of failure. The ranking of India is second among GEM participating economies. The data highlight that there is a fear of failure among youth to choose and to be entrepreneurs.

- Entrepreneurial intention is a very important part of the survey and highlights the possibility of people getting into business. The level of intentions among population keeps changing and compared to last year survey a persistent change has been observed. Entrepreneurial intention is 18.1% for this year and ranking of India is 21st among all 47 participating economies.

- However, about 82% of surveyed youth believe that starting a business is easy in India. The data has greatly improved for easiness to start a business in India. Out of the 47 economies who participated, India has ranked fourth on this parameter. It shows the ease of doing business in India.

- The rate of total early-stage entrepreneurship (TEA) in India has also improved from 5.4% in 2020–21 to 14.4% in 2021–22 and India now ranks 18th among 47 economies surveyed. Total early-stage entrepreneurial activity is an indicator of growth of the entrepreneurship development in the country.

- Among female adults, TEA has increased significantly as 12.3% of the total female population is engaged in entrepreneurship in India as compared to 16.3% of the male. The male–female difference still exists and needs to be worked on to improve female representation in the overall TEA of the country.

- The discussion for established business ownership is important and 8.5% of population is engaged in established business.

- The data of motivation for entrepreneurship is now more refined and very relevant to the entrepreneurship development in the country. People are majorly motivated by four different reasons to start a business. About 76% of the people in India want to start a business to make a difference in the world. The percentage is higher for youth in the age group of 18–34 years and it is 78% of males in the population. Another important category is to earn living because jobs are scarce and data shows that 91.5% of the population is motivated by this and 91% of youth in the age group of 18–34 years and 92% of youth in the age group of 35–64 years are motivated by the same objective of earn living because jobs are scarce.

- Among the youth of the country, 74% are motivated because they want to continue their family tradition and the same number of youths has reported that they are motivated to earn great wealth.

## 5.9 Key Takes from NES 2021–22

The national expert survey is the second essential survey conducted by GEM every year and this year it was conducted in 50 economies and results are summed up in a newly formed National Entrepreneurship Context Index (NECI). NECI identifies the capacity of the ecosystem of a particular country for the enhancement of the entrepreneurship in that country.

NES survey in India is based on 72 individual experts from the field of entrepreneurship, start-up, and academics. Experts from various fields directly or indirectly involved with the

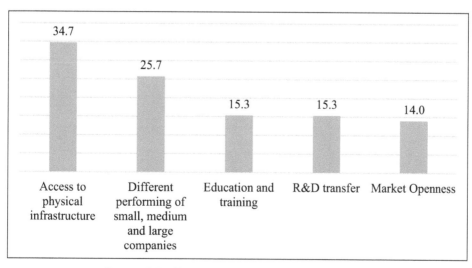

FIGURE 5.6   Fostering Factors for Entrepreneurship

*Source: GEM India Survey 2021–22*

entrepreneurship domain, suggest new things toward the improvement of the EFCs. The experts feel that the following fostering factors are facilitators for growth of entrepreneurship and development in India. Among the NES experts, 35% perceive access to physical infrastructure as one of most promising factors for the strengthening of the entrepreneurship ecosystem of the country. Experts also identified a few factors other then 'Physical Infrastructure' such as: 'differences among the firms or business', 'Education and training', 'R&D transfer', and 'Market Openness'.

Experts have also given their suggestions and recommendations for improving overall entrepreneurial ecosystem of the country. The four major points given by the experts are to improve financial support, education and training, government programs, and culture and social norms for entrepreneurship development in the country (Figure 5.7).

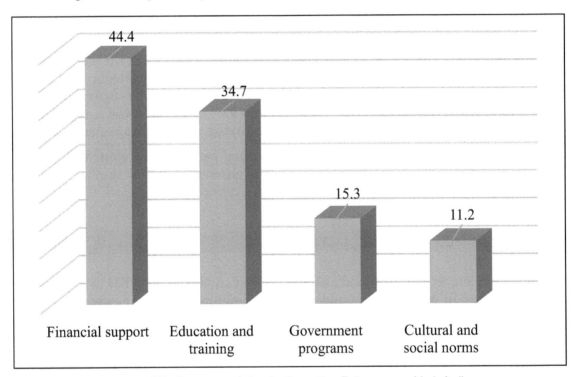

FIGURE 5.7   Recommendation for Promoting Entrepreneurship in India

Source: GEM India Survey 2021–22

# About Entrepreneurship Development Institute of India, Ahmedabad

The Entrepreneurship Development Institute of India (EDII), Ahmedabad was set up in 1983 as an autonomous and not-for-profit Institute with support of apex financial institutions - the IDBI Bank Ltd., IFCI Ltd., ICICI Bank Ltd. and State Bank of India (SBI). The Government of Gujarat pledged twenty-three acres of land on which stands the majestic and sprawling EDII Campus. EDII has been recognized as the CENTRE OF EXCELLENCE by the Ministry of Skill Development and Entrepreneurship, Govt. of India. The Institute has also been ranked as No. 1 under General (Non-Technical Category) by Atal Ranking of Institutions on Innovation Achievements (ARIIA)-2021, Ministry of Education, Govt. of India.

EDII moved on to adopt the role of a National Resource Institute in Entrepreneurship, and facilitated 12 state governments in setting up Entrepreneurship Development Centres/Institutes. The Institute's efforts in entrepreneurship training, education, research, MSME development, innovations and institutional building have been broad-based nationally and internationally too, with the setting up of Entrepreneurship Development Centres in Cambodia, Laos, Myanmar, Vietnam, Uzbekistan and Rwanda.

In consonance with the emphasis on startups and innovations, EDII hosted the Technology Business Incubator, CrAdLE – Centre for Advancing and Launching Enterprises in the year 2016, with the support of NSTEDB, DST, Govt. of India.

EDII has successfully brought about a change in the way entrepreneurship is perceived. The Institute has earned regional, national and international recognition for boosting entrepreneurship and start-ups across segments and sectors through innovative models and by intermediating creatively among stakeholders such as; new age potential entrepreneurs, minorities and the disadvantaged, existing entrepreneurs, incubation centre professionals, policy makers and venture capitalists. The Institute conducts a variety of programmes and projects through its 7 regional offices and 33 branch/project offices, under the *Departments of Policy Advocacy, Knowledge and Research, Entrepreneurship Education; Projects ( Government & Corporates); Business Development Services & National Outreach and Developing Economy Engagement.*

## The Departments at EDII:

### Policy Advocacy, Knowledge and Research

An Acknowledged Centre for Research in Entrepreneurship, Public Policy & Advocacy, this Department seeks to provide conceptual underpinnings to national and international policies, assist policy makers in their efforts to promote entrepreneurship opportunities and call upon government bodies and private organizations to integrate entrepreneurship in their development policies.

### Entrepreneurship Education

To augment the supply of new entrepreneurs, this Department aims at establishing entrepreneurship as an academic discipline and creating a conducive ecosystem for its growth. The Department offers industry relevant approved academic courses and programmes to strengthen entrepreneurship education, and undertakes curriculum development on entrepreneurship, thus establishing higher-order achievements in the domain.

### Department of Projects

Towards undertaking projects for economic and entrepreneurial transformations, this Department works for Corporates as well as Government. The Department aims to implement innovation-led projects, institutionalize S & T entrepreneurship, develop and enhance skills of potential/existing entrepreneurs in emerging sectors such as agriculture, food processing, handlooms, tourism, etc.

## Business Development Services and National Outreach

Considering the significance of fostering global competitiveness and growth of Micro, Small & Medium Enterprises (MSMEs), this Department targets providing business development services across regions and sectors, accelerating startups, facilitating growth of existing MSMEs and catering to the requirements of MSMEs across the country.

## Developing Economy Engagement

In order to facilitate developing countries to establish a flourishing entrepreneurial eco-system, this Department aims at institutionalizing entrepreneurship development initiatives in developing countries, sensitizing stakeholders in the entrepreneurial eco-system, in developing economies, about the ways and means of promoting and sustaining MSMEs, and training and skilling to ensure human resource development.

# Appendix

## List of GEM Indicators

| | |
|---|---|
| Knowing a Startup Entrepreneur | Percentage of adults aged 18–64 who personally know at least one person who has started a business in the past two years. |
| Perceived Opportunities | Percentage of adults aged 18–64 who agree' that they see good opportunities to start a business in the area where they live. |
| Ease of Starting a Business | Percentage of adults aged 18–64 who agree that it is easy to start a business in their country. |
| Perceived Capabilities | Percentage of adults 18–64 who agree that they have the required knowledge, skills and experience to start a business. |
| Fear of Failure Rate (opportunities) | Percentage of adults aged 18–64 who agree that they see good opportunities but would not start a business for fear it might fail. |
| Nascent Entrepreneurship Rate | Percentage of adults aged 18–64 who are currently nascent entrepreneurs, i.e. are actively involved in setting up a business they will own or co-own; this business has not yet paid salaries, wages, or any other payments to the owners for more than three months. |
| New Business Ownership Rate | Percentage of adults aged 18–64 who are currently owner-manager of a new business, i.e. who own and manage a running business that has paid salaries, wages, or any other payments to the owners for more than three months, but not for more than 42 months (3.5 years). |
| Total early-stage Entrepreneurial Activity (TEA) | Percentage of adults aged 18–64 who are either a nascent entrepreneur or owner-manager of a new business, i.e. the proportion of the adult population who are either starting or running a new business. |
| Established Business Ownership Rate (EBO) | Percentage of adults aged 18–64 who are currently owner-manager of an established business, i.e. who are owning and managing a running business that has paid salaries, wages, or any other payments to the owners for more than 42 month (3.5 years). |
| Business Services | Percentage of TEA in business services. |
| Consumer Services | Percentage of TEA in consumer services. |
| Entrepreneurial Employee Activity (EEA) | Percentage of adults aged 18–64 who, as employees, have been involved in entrepreneurial activities such as developing or launching new goods or services, or setting up a new business unit, a new establishment, or a subsidiary, in the last three years. |
| Motive for Starting a Business: "To make a difference in the world" | Percentage of TEA who agree that a reason for starting their business is "to make a difference in the world". |

---

1 In all cases, "agree" includes both somewhat and strongly agree.

| | |
|---|---|
| Motive for Starting a Business: "To build great wealth or very high income" | Percentage of TEA who agree that a reason for starting their business is "to build great wealth or a very high income". |
| Motive for Starting a Business: "To continue a family tradition" | Percentage of TEA who agree that a reason for starting their business is "to continue a family tradition". |
| Motive for Starting a Business: "To earn a living because jobs are scarce" | Percentage of TEA who agree that a reason for starting their business is "to earn a living because jobs are scarce". |
| High Growth Expectation Entrepreneurial Activity | Percentage of adults aged 18–64 starting or running a new business (TEA) who expect to employ six or more people five years from now. |
| Internationally Oriented Entrepreneurial Activity | Percentage of adults aged 18–64 involved in TEA who anticipate 25% or more revenue coming from outside their country. |
| Product/Services Impact (local/national/global) | Percentage adults aged 18–64 involved in TEA having products or services that are either new to the area, new to their country or new to the world. |
| Technology/Procedures Impact (local/national/global) | Percentage of adults aged 18–64 involved in TEA having technology or procedures that are either new to the area, new to their country or new to the world. |
| Digitization Rate | Percentage TEA who expect their business to use more digital technologies to sell their product or service in the next six months. |
| Social Impact Rate | Percentage of TEA who agree they always consider social implications when making decisions about the future of their business. |
| Environmental Impact Rate | Percentage of TEA who agree they always consider environmental implications when making decisions about the future of their business. |
| Business Exit Rate | Percentage of adults aged 18–64 who have exited a business in the past 12 months, either by selling, shutting down or otherwise discontinuing an owner/management relationship with that business. |

## Pandemic-Related Indicators

| | |
|---|---|
| Household Income Impact | Percentage of adults 18–64 who consider that the pandemic has led their household income to somewhat or strongly decrease. |
| More Difficult to Start a Business | Percentage of TEA who agree that, compared to one year ago, starting a business is somewhat or much more difficult. |
| Growth Expectations | Percentage of TEA whose growth expectations, compared to a year ago, are somewhat or much lower. |
| Pandemic Opportunities | Percentage of TEA who agree or strongly agree that the pandemic has provided new opportunities they wish to pursue. |

TABLE A1 Impact of pandemic on household income in past year (% of adults aged 18–64)

| | | | Strongly decrease | Somewhat decrease |
|---|---|---|---|---|
| Belarus | >$20k<$40k | Level B | 26.2 | 29.4 |
| Brazil | <$20k | Level C | 36.0 | 27.8 |
| Canada | >$40k | Level A | 13.3 | 22.3 |
| Chile | >$20k<$40k | Level B | 25.2 | 33.7 |
| Colombia | <$20k | Level C | 42.5 | 34.2 |
| Croatia | >$20k<$40k | Level B | 8.6 | 18.3 |
| Cyprus | >$20k<$40k | Level B | 13.7 | 27.1 |
| Dominican Republic | <$20k | Level C | 38.8 | 33.2 |
| Egypt | <$20k | Level C | 45.2 | 31.1 |
| Finland | >$40k | Level A | 4.6 | 13.1 |
| France | >$40k | Level A | 8.5 | 20.9 |
| Germany | >$40k | Level A | 4.3 | 16.5 |
| Greece | >$20k<$40k | Level B | 28.2 | 25.6 |
| Guatemala | <$20k | Level C | 30.7 | 34.8 |
| Hungary | >$20k<$40k | Level B | 11.4 | 21.2 |
| India | <$20k | Level C | 48.7 | 42.1 |
| Iran | <$20k | Level C | 13.4 | 35.6 |
| Ireland | >$40k | Level A | 11.0 | 22.6 |
| Israel | >$40k | Level A | 14.1 | 29.1 |
| Italy | >$40k | Level A | 15.5 | 26.0 |
| Japan | >$40k | Level A | 6.0 | 22.1 |
| Kazakhstan | >$20k<$40k | Level B | 37.1 | 55.7 |
| Latvia | >$20k<$40k | Level B | 9.4 | 18.7 |
| Luxembourg | >$40k | Level A | 5.7 | 15.0 |
| Morocco | <$20k | Level C | 42.0 | 32.8 |
| Netherlands | >$40k | Level A | 4.9 | 13.2 |
| Norway | >$40k | Level A | 2.6 | 8.8 |
| Oman | >$20k<$40k | Level B | 13.5 | 33.5 |
| Panama | >$20k<$40k | Level B | 40.5 | 37.5 |
| Poland | >$20k<$40k | Level B | 22.6 | 37.0 |

| | No substantial change | Somewhat increase | Strongly increase |
|---|---|---|---|
| Belarus | 40.5 | 2.5 | 1.3 |
| Brazil | 28.4 | 5.4 | 2.5 |
| Canada | 49.2 | 11.1 | 4.2 |
| Chile | 32.2 | 6.3 | 2.6 |
| Colombia | 17.3 | 3.5 | 2.5 |
| Croatia | 43.2 | 25.6 | 4.3 |
| Cyprus | 55.4 | 3.7 | 0.1 |
| Dominican Republic | 17.4 | 6.4 | 4.2 |
| Egypt | 19.9 | 2.2 | 1.6 |
| Finland | 72.4 | 8.1 | 1.9 |
| France | 62.1 | 6.7 | 1.8 |
| Germany | 68.0 | 10.2 | 0.9 |
| Greece | 43.9 | 1.7 | 0.6 |
| Guatemala | 25.8 | 5.9 | 2.8 |
| Hungary | 61.2 | 5.4 | 0.8 |
| India | 7.7 | 0.9 | 0.5 |
| Iran | 49.9 | 1.0 | 0.1 |
| Ireland | 53.0 | 10.7 | 2.7 |
| Israel | 51.3 | 4.7 | 0.9 |
| Italy | 53.1 | 4.0 | 1.4 |
| Japan | 65.5 | 5.2 | 1.2 |
| Kazakhstan | 6.7 | 0.6 | 0.0 |
| Latvia | 62.0 | 7.7 | 2.2 |
| Luxembourg | 71.9 | 5.5 | 1.9 |
| Morocco | 24.7 | 0.5 | 0.1 |
| Netherlands | 72.4 | 8.4 | 1.2 |
| Norway | 81.3 | 6.4 | 1.0 |
| Oman | 52.1 | 0.7 | 0.2 |
| Panama | 16.4 | 3.7 | 1.9 |
| Poland | 34.4 | 5.1 | 1.0 |

TABLE A1   (continued)

| | | | Strongly decrease | Somewhat decrease |
|---|---|---|---|---|
| Qatar | >$40k | Level A | 18.2 | 35.2 |
| Republic of Korea | >$40k | Level A | 1.5 | 32.0 |
| Romania | >$20k<$40k | Level B | 7.6 | 20.5 |
| Russian Federation | >$20k<$40k | Level B | 19.7 | 32.8 |
| Saudi Arabia | >$40k | Level A | 12.7 | 34.1 |
| Slovak Republic | >$20k<$40k | Level B | 17.3 | 37.9 |
| Slovenia | >$20k<$40k | Level B | 8.4 | 25.8 |
| South Africa | <$20k | Level C | 41.3 | 20.9 |
| Spain | >$20k<$40k | Level B | 15.0 | 25.2 |
| Sudan | <$20k | Level C | 61.4 | 18.5 |
| Sweden | >$40k | Level A | 5.6 | 15.1 |
| Switzerland | >$40k | Level A | 5.6 | 17.4 |
| Turkey | >$20k<$40k | Level B | 33.4 | 20.6 |
| United Arab Emirates | >$40k | Level A | 27.8 | 34.5 |
| United Kingdom | >$40k | Level A | 9.0 | 21.5 |
| United States | >$40k | Level A | 14.2 | 21.2 |
| Uruguay | >$20k<$40k | Level B | 25.6 | 33.4 |

| | No substantial change | Somewhat increase | Strongly increase |
|---|---|---|---|
| Qatar | 43.0 | 3.0 | 0.5 |
| Republic of Korea | 48.9 | 17.5 | 0.0 |
| Romania | 62.6 | 8.3 | 0.9 |
| Russian Federation | 43.6 | 3.1 | 0.8 |
| Saudi Arabia | 47.2 | 5.4 | 0.7 |
| Slovak Republic | 41.7 | 2.9 | 0.2 |
| Slovenia | 53.8 | 10.4 | 1.6 |
| South Africa | 27.5 | 6.0 | 4.3 |
| Spain | 55.4 | 3.7 | 0.6 |
| Sudan | 16.8 | 2.2 | 1.1 |
| Sweden | 59.8 | 17.1 | 2.3 |
| Switzerland | 70.5 | 5.7 | 0.8 |
| Turkey | 39.5 | 3.5 | 3.0 |
| United Arab Emirates | 28.3 | 4.9 | 4.4 |
| United Kingdom | 57.2 | 9.6 | 2.7 |
| United States | 49.5 | 10.3 | 4.8 |
| Uruguay | 34.3 | 4.2 | 2.4 |

TABLE A2   Entrepreneurial activity (% of adults aged 18–64)

*An equals sign (=) indicates that the ranking position is tied with another economy or economies*

| | Total early-stage Entrepreneurial Activity | | Established Business Ownership | | Entrepreneurial Employee Activity | |
|---|---|---|---|---|---|---|
| | Score | Rank/47 | Score | Rank/47 | Score | Rank/37 |
| Belarus | 13.5 | 20 | 5.5 | 26 | 2.4 | 22= |
| Brazil | 21.0 | 7 | 10.0 | 7 | 3.3 | 18 |
| Canada | 20.1 | 8 | 8.2 | 16 | 4.7 | 10 |
| Chile | 29.9 | 3 | 7.1 | 19= | 4.0 | 15 |
| Colombia | 15.7 | 15= | 1.8 | 47 | – | – |
| Croatia | 12.4 | 25 | 4.0 | 37 | 5.7 | 8= |
| Cyprus | 8.4 | 33 | 8.6 | 12 | 1.0 | 32 |
| Dominican Republic | 41.9 | 1 | 3.8 | 38 | – | – |
| Egypt | 9.2 | 30 | 3.6 | 40= | – | – |
| Finland | 7.9 | 35 | 8.9 | 9= | 6.6 | 4 |
| France | 7.7 | 36 | 3.6 | 40= | 2.8 | 21 |
| Germany | 6.9 | 38 | 5.0 | 30 | 3.4 | 17 |
| Greece | 5.5 | 43= | 14.7 | 2 | 1.5 | 28= |
| Guatemala | 28.3 | 4 | 12.7 | 3 | 1.1 | 31 |
| Hungary | 9.8 | 26= | 8.4 | 15 | 3.0 | 20 |
| India | 14.4 | 18 | 8.5 | 13= | 0.5 | 35 |
| Iran | 8.8 | 32 | 8.8 | 11 | 1.9 | 24= |
| Ireland | 12.5 | 24 | 6.9 | 21 | 5.7 | 8= |
| Israel | 9.6 | 29 | 3.3 | 45 | 5.8 | 6= |
| Italy | 4.8 | 45 | 4.5 | 33 | 3.2 | 19 |
| Japan | 6.3 | 41 | 4.8 | 32 | 1.7 | 26= |
| Kazakhstan | 19.9 | 9 | 12.1 | 4 | – | – |
| Latvia | 15.1 | 17 | 9.9 | 8 | 4.1 | 13= |
| Luxembourg | 7.3 | 37 | 3.6 | 40= | 4.6 | 11 |
| Morocco | 6.1 | 42 | 4.9 | 31 | – | – |
| Netherlands | 14.2 | 19 | 6.4 | 23= | 3.5 | 16 |
| Norway | 3.1 | 46 | 3.5 | 43 | 1.9 | 24= |
| Oman | 12.7 | 22 | 2.8 | 46 | – | – |

| | Total early-stage Entrepreneurial Activity | | Established Business Ownership | | Entrepreneurial Employee Activity | |
|---|---|---|---|---|---|---|
| | Score | Rank/47 | Score | Rank/47 | Score | Rank/37 |
| Panama | 21.8 | 6 | 3.7 | 39 | 1.7 | 26= |
| Poland | 2.0 | 47 | 11.1 | 5 | 0.8 | 33 |
| Qatar | 15.9 | 14 | 6.1 | 25 | 7.9 | 1 |
| Republic of Korea | 13.4 | 21 | 16.4 | 1 | 1.5 | 28= |
| Romania | 9.7 | 28 | 4.1 | 35= | 2.4 | 22= |
| Russian Federation | 8.3 | 34 | 3.4 | 44 | 0.3 | 36= |
| Saudi Arabia | 19.6 | 10 | 5.3 | 27= | 0.3 | 36= |
| Slovak Republic | 6.4 | 40 | 6.5 | 22 | 0.6 | 34 |
| Slovenia | 6.7 | 39 | 8.5 | 13= | 5.9 | 5 |
| South Africa | 17.5 | 11 | 5.2 | 29 | – | – |
| Spain | 5.5 | 43= | 7.2 | 18 | – | – |
| Sudan | 33.6 | 2 | 8.1 | 17 | 1.4 | 30 |
| Sweden | 9.0 | 31 | 4.3 | 34 | 5.8 | 6= |
| Switzerland | 9.8 | 26= | 7.1 | 19= | 7.1 | 3 |
| Turkey | 15.7 | 15= | 11.0 | 6 | – | – |
| United Arab Emirates | 16.5 | 12= | 6.4 | 23= | 7.8 | 2 |
| United Kingdom | 12.6 | 23 | 5.3 | 27= | 4.1 | 13= |
| United States | 16.5 | 12= | 8.9 | 9= | 4.5 | 12 |
| Uruguay | 23.1 | 5 | 4.1 | 35= | – | – |

Technical issues in data collection mean that the EEA variable is not available for a small number of economies in 2021.

TABLE A3    Public attitudes and perceptions (% of adults aged 18–64 somewhat or strongly agree)

| | Knowing someone who has started a business in the past two years | "There are good opportunities to start a business in the area where I live" | "In my country, it is easy to start a business" |
|---|---|---|---|
| Belarus | 61.3 | 25.0 | 34.5 |
| Brazil | 70.6 | 54.8 | 42.0 |
| Canada | 51.7 | 70.5 | 66.8 |
| Chile | 70.7 | 59.8 | 48.0 |
| Colombia | 58.2 | 38.1 | 29.0 |
| Croatia | 68.0 | 58.3 | 30.9 |
| Cyprus | 72.9 | 50.2 | 50.9 |
| Dominican Republic | 82.7 | 74.4 | 66.6 |
| Egypt | 30.8 | 73.2 | 72.4 |
| Finland | 64.1 | 61.0 | 69.6 |
| France | 46.3 | 52.1 | 52.0 |
| Germany | 39.9 | 48.2 | 38.2 |
| Greece | 32.6 | 48.6 | 35.1 |
| Guatemala | 71.1 | 69.1 | 48.8 |
| Hungary | 49.7 | 36.5 | 49.1 |
| India | 63.1 | 83.4 | 82.2 |
| Iran | 41.9 | 17.9 | 17.7 |
| Ireland | 57.5 | 57.3 | 58.9 |
| Israel | 63.5 | 45.8 | 13.7 |
| Italy | 41.1 | 34.7 | 16.6 |
| Japan | 20.1 | 11.7 | 29.7 |
| Kazakhstan | 53.4 | 51.4 | 52.4 |
| Latvia | 41.1 | 39.6 | 29.4 |
| Luxembourg | 43.0 | 54.1 | 64.1 |
| Morocco | 44.0 | 64.1 | 56.1 |
| Netherlands | 56.8 | 69.9 | 85.6 |
| Norway | 38.0 | 74.3 | 80.3 |

| | "You see good opportunities, but would not start a business for fear it might fail" (% of those seeing good opportunities) | "You personally have the knowledge, skills and experience required to start a business" | "Are you expecting to start a business in the next three years?" |
|---|---|---|---|
| Belarus | 56.0 | 52.0 | 24.1 |
| Brazil | 45.1 | 66.7 | 53.0 |
| Canada | 53.8 | 58.9 | 13.4 |
| Chile | 46.8 | 70.7 | 50.3 |
| Colombia | 48.7 | 56.2 | 20.9 |
| Croatia | 45.6 | 71.1 | 21.7 |
| Cyprus | 50.1 | 64.1 | 15.1 |
| Dominican Republic | 36.7 | 88.7 | 54.8 |
| Egypt | 53.0 | 65.8 | 55.3 |
| Finland | 44.5 | 42.8 | 9.7 |
| France | 44.1 | 48.6 | 14.5 |
| Germany | 37.9 | 37.1 | 5.8 |
| Greece | 51.5 | 53.1 | 9.6 |
| Guatemala | 41.5 | 76.3 | 45.0 |
| Hungary | 33.7 | 36.0 | 8.1 |
| India | 54.1 | 86.0 | 18.1 |
| Iran | 20.2 | 66.4 | 26.4 |
| Ireland | 49.9 | 57.8 | 15.2 |
| Israel | 46.6 | 37.5 | 17.5 |
| Italy | 45.3 | 44.7 | 9.4 |
| Japan | 47.9 | 12.3 | 3.2 |
| Kazakhstan | 12.1 | 65.4 | 55.3 |
| Latvia | 37.3 | 53.3 | 17.9 |
| Luxembourg | 43.0 | 52.9 | 13.2 |
| Morocco | 35.5 | 61.5 | 43.3 |
| Netherlands | 36.8 | 45.4 | 17.6 |
| Norway | 38.3 | 42.0 | 4.9 |

TABLE A3 (continued)

| | Knowing someone who has started a business in the past two years | "There are good opportunities to start a business in the area where I live" | "In my country, it is easy to start a business" |
|---|---|---|---|
| Oman | 69.4 | 67.7 | 44.5 |
| Panama | 45.3 | 46.3 | 49.1 |
| Poland | 54.0 | 72.5 | 64.3 |
| Qatar | 55.9 | 73.8 | 64.2 |
| Republic of Korea | 40.5 | 44.0 | 35.0 |
| Romania | 37.7 | 49.1 | 27.0 |
| Russian Federation | 59.8 | 33.5 | 32.5 |
| Saudi Arabia | 58.0 | 95.4 | 93.5 |
| Slovak Republic | 53.9 | 33.4 | 25.8 |
| Slovenia | 54.6 | 51.5 | 61.0 |
| South Africa | 37.6 | 57.9 | 67.6 |
| Spain | 38.1 | 30.0 | 35.9 |
| Sudan | 66.8 | 72.1 | 66.7 |
| Sweden | 55.1 | 79.6 | 82.6 |
| Switzerland | 54.7 | 54.7 | 68.9 |
| Turkey | 42.8 | 31.9 | 25.1 |
| United Arab Emirates | 54.6 | 73.5 | 74.4 |
| United Kingdom | 49.8 | 61.2 | 70.7 |
| United States | 58.8 | 63.2 | 66.9 |
| Uruguay | 54.5 | 58.4 | 37.7 |

| | "You see good opportunities, but would not start a business for fear it might fail" (% of those seeing good opportunities) | "You personally have the knowledge, skills and experience required to start a business" | "Are you expecting to start a business in the next three years?" |
|---|---|---|---|
| Oman | 24.6 | 59.2 | 53.2 |
| Panama | 45.6 | 69.8 | 44.1 |
| Poland | 43.5 | 60.1 | 2.9 |
| Qatar | 38.2 | 70.9 | 50.4 |
| Republic of Korea | 14.7 | 54.0 | 26.7 |
| Romania | 48.3 | 50.0 | 9.7 |
| Russian Federation | 48.2 | 34.5 | 9.7 |
| Saudi Arabia | 53.6 | 90.5 | 18.0 |
| Slovak Republic | 46.0 | 41.8 | 5.3 |
| Slovenia | 43.0 | 58.5 | 15.4 |
| South Africa | 53.0 | 69.7 | 20.0 |
| Spain | 51.0 | 49.8 | 7.7 |
| Sudan | 40.5 | 88.1 | 43.7 |
| Sweden | 43.6 | 49.9 | 13.1 |
| Switzerland | 30.4 | 49.6 | 13.4 |
| Turkey | 39.8 | 59.3 | 31.3 |
| United Arab Emirates | 49.7 | 65.1 | 35.9 |
| United Kingdom | 51.8 | 51.1 | 9.3 |
| United States | 42.6 | 64.6 | 14.8 |
| Uruguay | 48.2 | 69.8 | 33.0 |

TABLE A4  Attitudes and perceptions of entrepreneurs: % of Total early-stage Entrepreneurial Activity (TEA), % of Established Business Ownership (EBO), and % of Employee Entrepreneurial Activity (EEA)

| | The % of those starting or running a new or established business who agree/strongly agree that pandemic has provided new opportunities that they want to pursue/are pursuing | | | The % of those starting or running a new or established business who think starting a business is somewhat or much more difficult as a year ago | |
|---|---|---|---|---|---|
| | % TEA | % EBO | % EEA | % TEA | % EBO |
| Belarus | 30.4 | 19.6 | 36.1 | 66.1 | 58.8 |
| Brazil | 53.6 | 49.7 | 57.1 | 60.9 | 61.9 |
| Canada | 67.1 | 41.9 | 70.5 | 52.8 | 54.9 |
| Chile | 65.5 | 45.0 | 77.9 | 66.7 | 72.4 |
| Colombia | 55.9 | 44.3 | – | 58.4 | 78.8 |
| Croatia | 32.7 | 25.7 | 42.7 | 27.7 | 24.7 |
| Cyprus | 39.4 | 19.1 | 61.0 | 43.6 | 36.0 |
| Dominican Republic | 52.0 | 52.7 | – | 56.5 | 38.3 |
| Egypt | 43.5 | 34.3 | – | 40.7 | 38.0 |
| Finland | 28.8 | 22.4 | 60.3 | 13.3 | 21.0 |
| France | 39.9 | 30.9 | 54.0 | 35.2 | 33.0 |
| Germany | 36.5 | 30.9 | 30.1 | 39.0 | 40.7 |
| Greece | 28.9 | 14.9 | 39.4 | 41.1 | 56.9 |
| Guatemala | 51.5 | 38.7 | 64.5 | 58.5 | 67.7 |
| Hungary | 23.4 | 11.9 | 28.6 | 33.9 | 41.3 |
| India | 77.6 | 68.2 | 80.6 | 86.8 | 83.8 |
| Iran | 34.0 | 8.0 | 61.9 | 89.3 | 88.9 |
| Ireland | 60.5 | 52.6 | 66.6 | 51.8 | 55.3 |
| Israel | 50.0 | 25.9 | 47.4 | 40.9 | 45.9 |
| Italy | 46.3 | 23.4 | 36.0 | 47.0 | 57.6 |
| Japan | 28.0 | 17.4 | 37.9 | 49.1 | 52.3 |
| Kazakhstan | 32.5 | 19.2 | – | 67.3 | 75.5 |
| Latvia | 35.0 | 17.2 | 48.6 | 9.8 | 10.1 |
| Luxembourg | 46.8 | 30.7 | 36.5 | 38.8 | 44.2 |
| Morocco | 26.3 | 16.8 | – | 52.0 | 59.7 |

| | The % of those starting or running a new or established business who expect to use more digital technologies to sell products or services in the next six months | | The % of those starting or running a new or established business who agree/ strongly agree that they always consider the social implications of decisions | | The % of those starting or running a new or established business who agree/ strongly agree that they always consider the environmental implications of decisions | |
|---|---|---|---|---|---|---|
| | % TEA | % EBO | % TEA | % EBO | % TEA | % EBO |
| Belarus | 37.5 | 25.5 | 64.3 | 64.8 | 67.6 | 62.1 |
| Brazil | 83.6 | 66.2 | 89.9 | 84.5 | 84.1 | 85.7 |
| Canada | 55.4 | 38.3 | 80.3 | 64.8 | 72.2 | 62.6 |
| Chile | 77.0 | 51.0 | 88.0 | 87.2 | 90.9 | 94.4 |
| Colombia | 80.2 | 62.6 | 87.2 | 82.7 | 89.6 | 81.2 |
| Croatia | 57.3 | 52.5 | 78.7 | 78.7 | 81.9 | 85.4 |
| Cyprus | 53.1 | 46.2 | 68.0 | 72.3 | 65.9 | 72.7 |
| Dominican Republic | 74.5 | 64.4 | 81.2 | 73.5 | 79.7 | 64.9 |
| Egypt | 69.7 | 58.2 | 86.3 | 89.9 | 86.5 | 89.0 |
| Finland | 32.2 | 22.4 | 64.1 | 71.5 | 72.7 | 74.3 |
| France | 9.0 | 25.0 | 71.5 | 58.6 | 69.0 | 69.2 |
| Germany | 41.9 | 22.1 | 70.3 | 55.6 | 62.6 | 64.8 |
| Greece | 57.4 | 30.0 | 76.0 | 66.6 | 83.5 | 77.4 |
| Guatemala | 75.3 | 61.7 | 92.7 | 92.9 | 92.5 | 92.8 |
| Hungary | 28.3 | 18.0 | 74.5 | 60.9 | 86.3 | 83.7 |
| India | 59.3 | 48.8 | 89.6 | 85.0 | 81.9 | 80.5 |
| Iran | 54.2 | 26.9 | 69.1 | 51.7 | 60.0 | 40.3 |
| Ireland | 66.2 | 56.5 | 77.5 | 65.9 | 76.4 | 71.7 |
| Israel | 46.6 | 28.3 | 58.1 | 55.9 | 49.2 | 50.0 |
| Italy | 51.4 | 35.2 | 86.1 | 79.1 | 80.2 | 77.0 |
| Japan | 62.1 | 46.4 | 71.6 | 64.1 | 66.1 | 69.4 |
| Kazakhstan | 59.1 | 31.5 | 51.8 | 30.4 | 50.1 | 32.9 |
| Latvia | 49.6 | 28.8 | 82.1 | 75.2 | 83.1 | 77.1 |
| Luxembourg | 48.8 | 33.0 | 72.2 | 96.3 | 71.2 | 78.8 |
| Morocco | 66.6 | 34.8 | 85.3 | 73.7 | 85.1 | 80.8 |

TABLE A4 (continued)

| | The % of those starting or running a new or established business who agree/strongly agree that pandemic has provided new opportunities that they want to pursue/are pursuing | | | The % of those starting or running a new or established business who think starting a business is somewhat or much more difficult as a year ago | |
|---|---|---|---|---|---|
| | % TEA | % EBO | % EEA | % TEA | % EBO |
| Netherlands | 57.4 | 41.7 | 58.1 | 31.7 | 35.5 |
| Norway | 30.5 | 41.7 | 48.0 | 14.5 | 10.0 |
| Oman | 37.4 | 22.8 | | 37.2 | 37.0 |
| Panama | 53.7 | 44.0 | 77.8 | 62.5 | 62.7 |
| Poland | 24.8 | 21.6 | 44.2 | 41.9 | 23.8 |
| Qatar | 41.5 | 31.6 | 51.5 | 47.1 | 54.7 |
| Republic of Korea | 8.2 | 1.2 | 0.0 | 57.9 | 69.9 |
| Romania | 47.0 | 42.0 | 48.1 | 42.2 | 36.5 |
| Russian Federation | 21.0 | 11.4 | 0.0 | 49.6 | 62.9 |
| Saudi Arabia | 50.3 | 30.1 | 79.9 | 25.0 | 19.2 |
| Slovak Republic | 45.1 | 13.4 | 71.7 | 57.5 | 62.4 |
| Slovenia | 44.9 | 31.5 | 60.0 | 23.0 | 28.2 |
| South Africa | 48.9 | 54.2 | – | 59.2 | 56.2 |
| Spain | 40.8 | 24.5 | – | 48.5 | 48.3 |
| Sudan | 44.7 | 46.0 | 44.5 | 73.1 | 75.7 |
| Sweden | 38.6 | 26.1 | 57.4 | 18.6 | 15.6 |
| Switzerland | 36.6 | 40.3 | 55.0 | 30.6 | 35.6 |
| Turkey | 33.2 | 38.1 | – | 62.4 | 71.3 |
| United Arab Emirates | 59.9 | 63.6 | 58.7 | 32.2 | 29.3 |
| United Kingdom | 57.4 | 38.0 | 80.0 | 35.7 | 40.9 |
| United States | 52.6 | 40.1 | 55.4 | 35.4 | 39.0 |
| Uruguay | 42.2 | 27.1 | – | 47.0 | 39.3 |

Technical issues in data collection mean that the opportunity EEA variable is not available for a small number of economies in 2021, and that social and environmental implication variables are not available for South Africa.

| | The % of those starting or running a new or established business who expect to use more digital technologies to sell products or services in the next six months | | The % of those starting or running a new or established business who agree/ strongly agree that they always consider the social implications of decisions | | The % of those starting or running a new or established business who agree/ strongly agree that they always consider the environmental implications of decisions | |
|---|---|---|---|---|---|---|
| | % TEA | % EBO | % TEA | % EBO | % TEA | % EBO |
| Netherlands | 41.0 | 20.5 | 69.6 | 68.7 | 67.9 | 77.0 |
| Norway | 44.7 | 44.4 | 40.5 | 50.7 | 50.4 | 61.2 |
| Oman | 48.8 | 13.6 | 81.5 | 85.9 | 78.3 | 82.2 |
| Panama | 74.4 | 65.3 | 82.6 | 74.7 | 89.0 | 89.3 |
| Poland | 20.1 | 4.1 | 44.4 | 5.1 | 42.4 | 4.9 |
| Qatar | 70.6 | 61.9 | 87.5 | 88.1 | 86.4 | 85.9 |
| Republic of Korea | 51.0 | 62.0 | 60.5 | 63.5 | 57.5 | 72.9 |
| Romania | 28.0 | 20.1 | 81.4 | 71.3 | 83.9 | 82.3 |
| Russian Federation | 34.6 | 18.4 | 63.3 | 64.5 | 66.4 | 69.6 |
| Saudi Arabia | 47.7 | 23.1 | 81.9 | 64.3 | 77.9 | 59.0 |
| Slovak Republic | 17.2 | 16.7 | 77.7 | 76.1 | 67.3 | 74.9 |
| Slovenia | 45.6 | 30.9 | 85.6 | 82.7 | 92.0 | 89.0 |
| South Africa | 52.0 | 62.7 | – | – | – | – |
| Spain | 50.3 | 32.9 | 67.3 | 69.9 | 67.8 | 75.8 |
| Sudan | 59.9 | 57.3 | 82.1 | 85.1 | 81.0 | 90.1 |
| Sweden | 34.3 | 26.3 | 60.1 | 66.0 | 60.2 | 59.7 |
| Switzerland | 43.4 | 35.2 | 80.3 | 69.9 | 73.8 | 67.9 |
| Turkey | 55.2 | 50.7 | 79.0 | 78.9 | 89.5 | 89.4 |
| United Arab Emirates | 75.9 | 73.5 | 93.3 | 90.7 | 88.9 | 86.6 |
| United Kingdom | 62.7 | 43.8 | 73.3 | 72.0 | 72.7 | 67.8 |
| United States | 60.8 | 34.3 | 76.0 | 61.6 | 75.6 | 67.0 |
| Uruguay | 64.5 | 31.4 | 87.2 | 72.5 | 85.7 | 93.5 |

TABLE A5   Entrepreneurial activity by age, gender and education (% of adults aged 18–64)

| | Total early-stage Entrepreneurial Activity (TEA) by gender | | Total early-stage Entrepreneurial Activity (TEA) by age group | | Total early-stage Entrepreneurial Activity (TEA) for graduates and for non-graduates | |
|---|---|---|---|---|---|---|
| | TEA male | TEA female | 18–34 | 35–64 | % TEA graduates | % TEA non-graduates |
| Belarus | 14.2 | 12.9 | 17.4 | 11.6 | 17.1 | 9.8 |
| Brazil | 23.3 | 18.7 | 22.9 | 19.6 | 26.5 | 19.4 |
| Canada | 24.4 | 15.8 | 31.3 | 14.1 | 20.9 | 17.4 |
| Chile | 34.7 | 25.3 | 32.9 | 27.8 | 31.3 | 27.3 |
| Colombia | 17.4 | 14.1 | 16.8 | 14.8 | 16.7 | 14.3 |
| Croatia | 15.5 | 9.2 | 18.1 | 9.3 | 16.3 | 9.8 |
| Cyprus | 10.8 | 6.1 | 8.1 | 8.5 | 9.7 | 5.7 |
| Dominican Republic | 40.1 | 43.8 | 41.6 | 42.2 | 42.7 | 41.0 |
| Egypt | 12.5 | 5.7 | 10.7 | 7.4 | 12.3 | 8.1 |
| Finland | 9.4 | 6.4 | 8.4 | 7.6 | 8.2 | 7.6 |
| France | 8.4 | 7.1 | 9.5 | 6.8 | 10.0 | 4.7 |
| Germany | 8.4 | 5.3 | 9.4 | 5.7 | 8.5 | 5.6 |
| Greece | 6.5 | 4.6 | 6.8 | 4.7 | 5.7 | 5.4 |
| Guatemala | 32.9 | 23.9 | 31.2 | 24.6 | 33.7 | 27.9 |
| Hungary | 12.1 | 7.5 | 11.7 | 8.7 | 10.7 | 9.3 |
| India | 16.3 | 12.3 | 14.2 | 14.5 | 17.1 | 9.7 |
| Iran | 10.4 | 7.1 | 9.2 | 8.4 | 9.6 | 7.6 |
| Ireland | 13.7 | 11.3 | 16.7 | 10.2 | 13.4 | 10.5 |
| Israel | 10.4 | 8.8 | 9.3 | 9.7 | 9.5 | 9.8 |
| Italy | 6.2 | 3.5 | 8.3 | 3.4 | 9.7 | 3.5 |
| Japan | 8.5 | 4.0 | 6.1 | 6.4 | 5.5 | 7.4 |
| Kazakhstan | 18.5 | 21.3 | 21.2 | 19.0 | 19.7 | 20.8 |
| Latvia | 18.2 | 12.0 | 22.0 | 11.9 | 12.4 | 16.2 |
| Luxembourg | 9.3 | 5.1 | 9.7 | 5.9 | 9.6 | 3.0 |
| Morocco | 5.9 | 6.3 | 6.3 | 5.8 | 5.4 | 6.6 |
| Netherlands | 15.5 | 13.0 | 15.6 | 13.5 | 17.5 | 12.6 |
| Norway | 4.4 | 1.8 | 2.0 | 3.7 | 2.7 | 3.7 |

| | Total early-stage Entrepreneurial Activity (TEA) by gender | | Total early-stage Entrepreneurial Activity (TEA) by age group | | Total early-stage Entrepreneurial Activity (TEA) for graduates and for non-graduates | |
|---|---|---|---|---|---|---|
| | TEA male | TEA female | 18–34 | 35–64 | % TEA graduates | % TEA non-graduates |
| Oman | 13.5 | 11.9 | 15.0 | 9.4 | 14.0 | 11.1 |
| Panama | 23.2 | 20.3 | 23.1 | 20.7 | 23.6 | 18.9 |
| Poland | 2.4 | 1.7 | 3.0 | 1.5 | 2.1 | 1.7 |
| Qatar | 17.2 | 10.5 | 15.9 | 15.8 | 17.0 | 12.6 |
| Republic of Korea | 15.9 | 10.7 | 10.9 | 14.5 | 14.1 | 12.4 |
| Romania | 9.8 | 9.6 | 11.3 | 8.9 | 10.7 | 6.0 |
| Russian Federation | 10.2 | 6.6 | 10.7 | 7.1 | 8.7 | 6.9 |
| Saudi Arabia | 20.1 | 19.0 | 18.9 | 20.2 | 18.9 | 21.7 |
| Slovak Republic | 7.8 | 5.0 | 8.4 | 5.4 | 7.3 | 6.0 |
| Slovenia | 7.2 | 6.1 | 12.3 | 4.3 | 8.0 | 5.5 |
| South Africa | 18.8 | 16.2 | 19.2 | 15.3 | 17.2 | 17.7 |
| Spain | 5.4 | 5.6 | 5.3 | 5.6 | 7.8 | 3.8 |
| Sudan | 40.8 | 26.4 | 33.5 | 33.7 | 36.0 | 32.3 |
| Sweden | 11.8 | 6.0 | 9.2 | 8.8 | 9.4 | 8.4 |
| Switzerland | 12.3 | 7.2 | 8.9 | 10.3 | 11.7 | 6.6 |
| Turkey | 21.1 | 10.3 | 16.3 | 15.2 | 15.5 | 15.7 |
| United Arab Emirates | 20.1 | 8.2 | 16.1 | 17.0 | 16.4 | 17.1 |
| United Kingdom | 14.2 | 10.9 | 16.0 | 10.6 | 13.3 | 11.8 |
| United States | 17.8 | 15.2 | 18.9 | 15.1 | 15.9 | 18.5 |
| Uruguay | 25.9 | 20.2 | 26.3 | 20.9 | 26.2 | 22.5 |

TABLE A6    Sector distribution of new entrepreneurial activity (% of Total early-stage Entrepreneurial Activity)

| | Business-oriented services | Consumer-oriented services | Extractive sector | Transforming sector |
|---|---|---|---|---|
| Belarus | 20.3 | 39.0 | 7.8 | 33.0 |
| Brazil | 12.1 | 61.4 | 2.5 | 24.0 |
| Canada | 25.5 | 51.9 | 3.4 | 19.2 |
| Chile | 16.3 | 56.9 | 4.0 | 22.8 |
| Colombia | 17.0 | 59.0 | 0.7 | 23.3 |
| Croatia | 25.6 | 36.6 | 11.2 | 26.6 |
| Cyprus | 16.7 | 58.6 | 3.2 | 21.5 |
| Dominican Republic | 11.5 | 75.2 | 0.8 | 12.5 |
| Egypt | 6.7 | 44.6 | 9.5 | 39.2 |
| Finland | 31.6 | 36.0 | 12.1 | 20.3 |
| France | 35.9 | 41.2 | 4.0 | 18.9 |
| Germany | 29.0 | 50.4 | 2.6 | 18.1 |
| Greece | 17.3 | 42.7 | 12.4 | 27.6 |
| Guatemala | 5.2 | 72.9 | 5.5 | 16.4 |
| Hungary | 16.9 | 42.9 | 11.5 | 28.7 |
| India | 1.7 | 71.3 | 8.2 | 18.8 |
| Iran | 16.6 | 44.4 | 4.8 | 34.2 |
| Ireland | 21.8 | 54.5 | 5.1 | 18.6 |
| Israel | 40.4 | 48.1 | 0.6 | 10.9 |
| Italy | 36.9 | 41.0 | 5.4 | 16.7 |
| Japan | 25.2 | 56.3 | 2.8 | 15.6 |
| Kazakhstan | 12.1 | 56.4 | 6.0 | 25.5 |
| Latvia | 24.7 | 36.5 | 8.4 | 30.4 |
| Luxembourg | 43.8 | 35.7 | 2.7 | 17.8 |
| Morocco | 8.5 | 55.6 | 5.5 | 30.4 |
| Netherlands | 26.8 | 57.1 | 0.5 | 15.6 |
| Norway | 32.6 | 44.1 | 7.4 | 16.0 |
| Oman | 14.5 | 57.8 | 8.3 | 19.4 |
| Panama | 15.7 | 61.9 | 4.6 | 17.8 |

| | Business-oriented services | Consumer-oriented services | Extractive sector | Transforming sector |
|---|---|---|---|---|
| Poland | 21.5 | 46.8 | 8.2 | 23.4 |
| Qatar | 17.8 | 46.2 | 2.3 | 33.7 |
| Republic of Korea | 16.6 | 56.0 | 3.0 | 24.4 |
| Romania | 14.6 | 44.1 | 12.9 | 28.4 |
| Russian Federation | 15.4 | 42.6 | 4.9 | 37.0 |
| Saudi Arabia | 3.8 | 86.9 | 0.4 | 8.9 |
| Slovak Republic | 17.0 | 52.1 | 2.4 | 28.5 |
| Slovenia | 30.0 | 41.7 | 2.6 | 25.7 |
| South Africa | 8.8 | 68.6 | 4.6 | 18.1 |
| Spain | 34.1 | 44.4 | 3.4 | 18.1 |
| Sudan | 4.3 | 51.1 | 20.7 | 23.9 |
| Sweden | 34.1 | 39.3 | 8.3 | 18.3 |
| Switzerland | 42.2 | 36.6 | 2.7 | 18.5 |
| Turkey | 11.4 | 44.4 | 12.0 | 32.2 |
| United Arab Emirates | 23.2 | 45.6 | 1.3 | 30.0 |
| United Kingdom | 34.5 | 52.1 | 1.9 | 11.5 |
| United States | 32.6 | 44.6 | 3.9 | 18.9 |
| Uruguay | 15.1 | 54.9 | 5.7 | 24.4 |

TABLE A7   Business exits, and reason for exit (positive, negative [non-COVID] and COVID-related), % of adults aged 18–64

| | Business exits | Positive | Negative, not including COVID-19 pandemic | COVID-19 pandemic |
|---|---|---|---|---|
| Belarus | 7.4 | 1.1 | 5.5 | 0.7 |
| Brazil | 11.3 | 1.0 | 5.8 | 4.5 |
| Canada | 11.8 | 4.4 | 5.6 | 1.8 |
| Chile | 9.0 | 1.6 | 4.4 | 3.0 |
| Colombia | 6.6 | 0.7 | 2.7 | 3.2 |
| Croatia | 4.4 | 1.2 | 2.3 | 1.0 |
| Cyprus | 5.7 | 1.3 | 3.3 | 1.1 |
| Dominican Republic | 15.0 | 2.4 | 7.9 | 4.6 |
| Egypt | 10.9 | 0.5 | 6.7 | 3.8 |
| Finland | 1.9 | 0.7 | 0.9 | 0.3 |
| France | 2.6 | 0.8 | 1.3 | 0.5 |
| Germany | 3.3 | 1.0 | 1.9 | 0.4 |
| Greece | 2.0 | 0.5 | 1.4 | 0.1 |
| Guatemala | 9.1 | 1.1 | 4.7 | 3.3 |
| Hungary | 2.1 | 0.4 | 1.3 | 0.4 |
| India | 8.0 | 1.3 | 4.0 | 2.6 |
| Iran | 5.8 | 0.3 | 4.6 | 0.9 |
| Ireland | 7.0 | 2.0 | 3.4 | 1.6 |
| Israel | 4.6 | 0.9 | 2.5 | 1.2 |
| Italy | 1.3 | 0.3 | 0.9 | 0.1 |
| Japan | 1.6 | 0.4 | 0.8 | 0.4 |
| Kazakhstan | 19.2 | 0.9 | 15.6 | 2.8 |
| Latvia | 3.1 | 0.4 | 2.2 | 0.6 |
| Luxembourg | 4.2 | 0.9 | 2.8 | 0.4 |
| Morocco | 4.6 | 0.3 | 3.8 | 0.5 |
| Netherlands | 5.9 | 1.6 | 3.6 | 0.7 |
| Norway | 0.8 | 0.1 | 0.6 | 0.2 |
| Oman | 13.7 | 1.4 | 6.5 | 5.8 |
| Panama | 11.4 | 1.0 | 4.5 | 5.8 |

| | Business exits | Positive | Negative, not including COVID-19 pandemic | COVID-19 pandemic |
|---|---|---|---|---|
| Poland | 4.5 | 1.2 | 1.0 | 2.3 |
| Qatar | 11.5 | 0.7 | 4.8 | 6.0 |
| Republic of Korea | 3.7 | 0.3 | 3.3 | 0.2 |
| Romania | 2.6 | 0.2 | 1.3 | 1.2 |
| Russian Federation | 3.9 | 0.6 | 2.6 | 0.7 |
| Saudi Arabia | 8.6 | 1.6 | 4.7 | 2.3 |
| Slovak Republic | 3.6 | 0.6 | 1.6 | 1.5 |
| Slovenia | 3.0 | 0.9 | 1.2 | 0.9 |
| South Africa | 14.1 | 2.0 | 8.7 | 3.4 |
| Spain | 2.2 | 0.6 | 1.1 | 0.5 |
| Sudan | 13.1 | 2.8 | 9.9 | 0.4 |
| Sweden | 3.6 | 1.3 | 2.2 | 0.1 |
| Switzerland | 2.9 | 0.7 | 1.7 | 0.5 |
| Turkey | 8.2 | 0.6 | 5.8 | 1.8 |
| United Arab Emirates | 10.3 | 1.1 | 6.0 | 3.2 |
| United Kingdom | 2.7 | 0.6 | 1.7 | 0.4 |
| United States | 6.4 | 1.3 | 3.7 | 1.4 |
| Uruguay | 9.7 | 1.3 | 6.6 | 1.8 |

TABLE A8   Entrepreneurial expectations and scope (% of adults aged 18–64)

| | The % of adults (aged 18–64) starting or running a new business and their job expectations in five years' time | | | The % of adults (aged 18–64) starting or running a new business and anticipating 25% or more revenue from outside their country |
|---|---|---|---|---|
| | 0 jobs | 1–5 jobs | 6 or more jobs | |
| Belarus | 6.5 | 3.1 | 3.9 | 2.6 |
| Brazil | 7.1 | 7.5 | 6.4 | 0.2 |
| Canada | 11.6 | 4.9 | 3.6 | 5.9 |
| Chile | 4.0 | 15.8 | 10.1 | 0.2 |
| Colombia | 1.2 | 7.3 | 7.2 | 0.9 |
| Croatia | 4.2 | 4.4 | 3.7 | 2.0 |
| Cyprus | 3.1 | 4.5 | 0.8 | 1.2 |
| Dominican Republic | 33.8 | 5.8 | 2.4 | 6.1 |
| Egypt | 3.5 | 2.5 | 3.2 | 0.6 |
| Finland | 4.9 | 2.2 | 0.8 | 0.7 |
| France | 3.5 | 2.4 | 1.8 | 1.0 |
| Germany | 3.8 | 2.1 | 1.0 | 1.1 |
| Greece | 1.8 | 2.8 | 1.0 | 1.4 |
| Guatemala | 6.0 | 14.8 | 7.5 | 0.3 |
| Hungary | 4.4 | 4.2 | 1.2 | 0.8 |
| India | 6.7 | 6.9 | 0.7 | 0.1 |
| Iran | 3.1 | 2.9 | 2.8 | 0.2 |
| Ireland | 5.0 | 3.9 | 3.5 | 3.0 |
| Israel | 5.4 | 2.6 | 1.5 | 1.5 |
| Italy | 2.5 | 1.3 | 1.0 | 0.5 |
| Japan | 3.0 | 2.0 | 1.3 | 0.5 |
| Kazakhstan | 9.6 | 5.0 | 5.4 | 0.2 |
| Latvia | 6.1 | 4.7 | 4.3 | 2.8 |
| Luxembourg | 1.9 | 3.4 | 2.0 | 1.7 |
| Morocco | 1.4 | 2.7 | 2.0 | 0.4 |
| Netherlands | 4.4 | 6.2 | 3.6 | 2.9 |

| | The proportion of adults starting a new business with products or services that are either new to their area, new to their country or new to the world | | | The proportion of adults starting or running a new business using technology or processes that are either new to their area, new to their country or new to the world | | |
|---|---|---|---|---|---|---|
| | New to their area | New to their country | New to the world | New to their area | New to their country | New to the world |
| Belarus | 1.6 | 0.7 | 0.2 | 1.8 | 0.4 | 0.4 |
| Brazil | 3.8 | 0.3 | 0.3 | 3.0 | 0.4 | 0.0 |
| Canada | 6.2 | 2.9 | 1.3 | 5.8 | 2.7 | 0.9 |
| Chile | 10.0 | 3.1 | 2.4 | 8.0 | 2.3 | 1.2 |
| Colombia | 4.3 | 1.8 | 0.5 | 3.9 | 1.5 | 0.5 |
| Croatia | 2.2 | 2.0 | 0.9 | 1.5 | 1.9 | 0.5 |
| Cyprus | 1.3 | 1.1 | 0.0 | 2.0 | 1.0 | 0.1 |
| Dominican Republic | 7.0 | 3.6 | 0.7 | 6.5 | 3.2 | 0.7 |
| Egypt | 2.3 | 0.6 | 0.1 | 2.4 | 0.5 | 0.0 |
| Finland | 0.5 | 0.8 | 0.7 | 0.6 | 0.8 | 0.5 |
| France | 1.3 | 0.9 | 0.4 | 1.3 | 0.7 | 0.4 |
| Germany | 1.1 | 0.7 | 0.3 | 0.9 | 0.5 | 0.2 |
| Greece | 0.8 | 0.7 | 0.3 | 0.7 | 0.7 | 0.1 |
| Guatemala | 8.7 | 0.8 | 0.5 | 7.0 | 1.0 | 0.9 |
| Hungary | 1.8 | 0.6 | 0.2 | 1.5 | 0.7 | 0.0 |
| India | 2.4 | 0.2 | 0.1 | 2.5 | 0.2 | 0.1 |
| Iran | 1.1 | 0.5 | 0.2 | 0.5 | 0.4 | 0.1 |
| Ireland | 3.5 | 1.2 | 0.7 | 3.3 | 1.2 | 0.6 |
| Israel | 1.4 | 0.7 | 0.3 | 0.6 | 0.4 | 0.4 |
| Italy | 1.1 | 0.5 | 0.3 | 0.8 | 0.6 | 0.2 |
| Japan | 1.1 | 1.2 | 0.4 | 1.2 | 1.1 | 0.6 |
| Kazakhstan | 0.4 | 0.1 | 0.1 | 1.0 | 0.1 | 0.0 |
| Latvia | 1.0 | 0.8 | 1.1 | 0.6 | 1.1 | 0.6 |
| Luxembourg | 1.0 | 2.0 | 0.9 | 0.4 | 0.8 | 1.0 |
| Morocco | 0.9 | 0.2 | 0.0 | 0.6 | 0.2 | 0.0 |
| Netherlands | 2.7 | 1.6 | 1.2 | 2.4 | 1.8 | 0.8 |

TABLE A8   (continued)

| | The % of adults (aged 18–64) starting or running a new business and their job expectations in five years' time | | | The % of adults (aged 18–64) starting or running a new business and anticipating 25% or more revenue from outside their country |
|---|---|---|---|---|
| | 0 jobs | 1–5 jobs | 6 or more jobs | |
| Norway | 1.1 | 1.3 | 0.7 | 0.2 |
| Oman | 8.5 | 1.9 | 2.3 | 0.5 |
| Panama | 2.4 | 11.1 | 8.2 | 0.7 |
| Poland | 0.6 | 1.0 | 0.4 | 0.1 |
| Qatar | 4.1 | 2.0 | 9.8 | 1.5 |
| Republic of Korea | 3.9 | 5.4 | 4.1 | 0.7 |
| Romania | 5.1 | 3.0 | 1.6 | 0.4 |
| Russian Federation | 2.7 | 2.3 | 3.4 | 0.3 |
| Saudi Arabia | 3.2 | 11.5 | 4.9 | 0.3 |
| Slovak Republic | 3.8 | 2.2 | 0.4 | 0.1 |
| Slovenia | 2.8 | 2.6 | 1.2 | 1.0 |
| South Africa | 7.3 | 4.9 | 5.3 | 1.4 |
| Spain | 2.8 | 2.1 | 0.6 | 0.6 |
| Sudan | 20.4 | 7.7 | 5.5 | 1.5 |
| Sweden | 5.5 | 2.6 | 0.8 | 0.9 |
| Switzerland | 4.3 | 3.3 | 2.2 | 2.1 |
| Turkey | 3.6 | 3.4 | 8.7 | 2.5 |
| United Arab Emirates | 2.1 | 2.4 | 12.0 | 4.4 |
| United Kingdom | 5.7 | 4.5 | 2.4 | 2.7 |
| United States | 6.0 | 5.8 | 4.6 | 0.9 |
| Uruguay | 8.4 | 9.1 | 5.6 | 0.9 |

| | The proportion of adults starting a new business with products or services that are either new to their area, new to their country or new to the world | | | The proportion of adults starting or running a new business using technology or processes that are either new to their area, new to their country or new to the world | | |
|---|---|---|---|---|---|---|
| | New to their area | New to their country | New to the world | New to their area | New to their country | New to the world |
| Norway | 0.6 | 0.3 | 0.1 | 0.2 | 0.0 | 0.1 |
| Oman | 1.8 | 0.5 | 0.1 | 1.1 | 0.4 | 0.0 |
| Panama | 5.1 | 1.5 | 0.7 | 6.1 | 1.5 | 0.7 |
| Poland | 0.2 | 0.1 | 0.0 | 0.3 | 0.1 | 0.0 |
| Qatar | 1.7 | 3.4 | 0.3 | 1.9 | 4.0 | 0.5 |
| Republic of Korea | 1.3 | 1.9 | 0.4 | 1.1 | 1.4 | 0.3 |
| Romania | 1.1 | 0.8 | 0.2 | 1.1 | 0.8 | 0.1 |
| Russian Federation | 1.0 | 0.1 | 0.2 | 0.9 | 0.1 | 0.1 |
| Saudi Arabia | 1.8 | 0.4 | 0.1 | 1.7 | 0.5 | 0.1 |
| Slovak Republic | 1.4 | 0.2 | 0.0 | 0.8 | 0.3 | 0.1 |
| Slovenia | 1.0 | 1.0 | 0.5 | 1.0 | 0.8 | 0.3 |
| South Africa | 4.0 | 0.9 | 0.3 | 3.2 | 0.9 | 0.3 |
| Spain | 0.8 | 0.4 | 0.3 | 0.8 | 0.5 | 0.3 |
| Sudan | 1.6 | 0.5 | 0.0 | 2.2 | 0.5 | 0.0 |
| Sweden | 1.0 | 0.7 | 0.6 | 0.9 | 1.0 | 0.5 |
| Switzerland | 1.6 | 1.3 | 1.1 | 0.8 | 1.0 | 0.9 |
| Turkey | 3.8 | 3.4 | 1.5 | 4.6 | 2.4 | 0.8 |
| United Arab Emirates | 3.0 | 2.7 | 1.3 | 3.1 | 3.1 | 1.2 |
| United Kingdom | 2.1 | 0.8 | 1.2 | 1.6 | 0.6 | 0.7 |
| United States | 1.9 | 1.0 | 1.6 | 1.7 | 1.0 | 1.1 |
| Uruguay | 3.5 | 1.7 | 0.6 | 3.8 | 1.8 | 1.3 |

TABLE A9    The motivation to start a business (% of Total early-stage Entrepreneurial Activity who somewhat or strongly agree)

| | "To make a difference in the world" | "To build great wealth or very high income" | "To continue a family tradition" | "To earn a living because jobs are scarce" |
|---|---|---|---|---|
| Belarus | 25.5 | 76.2 | 15.1 | 71.5 |
| Brazil | 75.7 | 56.5 | 32.0 | 76.8 |
| Canada | 70.4 | 68.4 | 50.0 | 70.7 |
| Chile | 56.6 | 53.5 | 33.6 | 73.9 |
| Colombia | 64.6 | 64.3 | 43.6 | 78.8 |
| Croatia | 38.7 | 51.3 | 28.5 | 65.7 |
| Cyprus | 32.2 | 81.3 | 13.7 | 72.8 |
| Dominican Republic | 72.1 | 64.4 | 37.6 | 72.9 |
| Egypt | 63.4 | 72.4 | 49.5 | 86.9 |
| Finland | 40.1 | 33.4 | 24.3 | 47.9 |
| France | 25.8 | 39.4 | 22.9 | 51.2 |
| Germany | 39.4 | 43.7 | 24.2 | 40.9 |
| Greece | 29.9 | 50.4 | 39.7 | 63.2 |
| Guatemala | 80.7 | 75.8 | 49.2 | 91.7 |
| Hungary | 61.7 | 32.5 | 21.0 | 66.8 |
| India | 75.9 | 73.4 | 74.3 | 91.5 |
| Iran | 36.7 | 92.9 | 17.3 | 64.1 |
| Ireland | 57.8 | 59.0 | 29.0 | 56.0 |
| Israel | 36.9 | 74.9 | 15.0 | 49.8 |
| Italy | 21.5 | 53.4 | 22.8 | 61.4 |
| Japan | 37.3 | 42.1 | 31.9 | 40.1 |
| Kazakhstan | 0.3 | 91.3 | 8.7 | 39.8 |
| Latvia | 36.9 | 37.1 | 24.2 | 65.3 |
| Luxembourg | 56.9 | 38.6 | 27.7 | 32.9 |
| Morocco | 17.6 | 46.5 | 22.3 | 87.1 |
| Netherlands | 52.7 | 41.8 | 24.5 | 44.1 |
| Norway | 39.2 | 37.4 | 23.0 | 26.5 |
| Oman | 43.7 | 78.2 | 26.0 | 89.7 |

| | "To make a difference in the world" | | "To build great wealth or very high income" | | "To continue a family tradition" | | "To earn a living because jobs are scarce" | |
|---|---|---|---|---|---|---|---|---|
| | 18–34 | 35–64 | 18–34 | 35–64 | 18–34 | 35–64 | 18–34 | 35–64 |
| Belarus | 28.9 | 22.9 | 84.0 | 70.4 | 12.5 | 16.9 | 62.6 | 78.1 |
| Brazil | 80.4 | 71.8 | 65.5 | 48.9 | 27.4 | 35.9 | 75.8 | 77.7 |
| Canada | 71.0 | 69.7 | 70.7 | 65.8 | 56.1 | 43.0 | 69.7 | 71.9 |
| Chile | 60.5 | 53.3 | 57.9 | 49.8 | 32.1 | 34.9 | 71.4 | 76.0 |
| Colombia | 70.1 | 59.4 | 65.8 | 62.9 | 44.1 | 43.1 | 80.0 | 77.8 |
| Croatia | 44.9 | 32.1 | 58.9 | 43.4 | 26.3 | 30.7 | 55.4 | 76.4 |
| Cyprus | 38.4 | 27.7 | 87.8 | 76.7 | 10.7 | 15.9 | 72.7 | 72.8 |
| Dominican Republic | 70.6 | 73.4 | 66.5 | 62.7 | 38.5 | 36.8 | 77.1 | 69.4 |
| Egypt | 63.1 | 64.0 | 80.0 | 58.6 | 50.8 | 47.2 | 85.6 | 89.3 |
| Finland | 41.2 | 39.5 | 36.9 | 31.4 | 27.6 | 22.2 | 43.3 | 50.6 |
| France | 26.9 | 25.0 | 49.4 | 32.0 | 26.2 | 20.6 | 55.3 | 48.3 |
| Germany | 40.1 | 38.8 | 54.4 | 35.2 | 25.7 | 23.1 | 34.5 | 45.9 |
| Greece | 32.8 | 27.0 | 43.9 | 56.7 | 42.8 | 36.7 | 51.4 | 74.3 |
| Guatemala | 82.6 | 77.5 | 79.2 | 70.2 | 48.8 | 49.8 | 91.6 | 91.9 |
| Hungary | 64.4 | 59.8 | 38.6 | 28.2 | 20.5 | 21.3 | 62.2 | 70.0 |
| India | 75.1 | 76.7 | 70.4 | 76.6 | 70.2 | 78.4 | 90.9 | 92.1 |
| Iran | 36.5 | 36.8 | 94.5 | 91.2 | 16.4 | 18.3 | 65.4 | 62.8 |
| Ireland | 63.8 | 52.4 | 65.5 | 53.3 | 31.4 | 26.9 | 57.9 | 54.3 |
| Israel | 33.3 | 39.4 | 79.0 | 72.0 | 9.3 | 18.9 | 50.7 | 49.2 |
| Italy | 24.7 | 18.3 | 55.3 | 51.6 | 14.2 | 31.6 | 56.6 | 66.2 |
| Japan | 40.1 | 36.1 | 69.5 | 31.4 | 38.1 | 29.5 | 41.4 | 39.6 |
| Kazakhstan | 0.6 | 0.0 | 90.8 | 91.7 | 11.6 | 6.4 | 35.0 | 43.7 |
| Latvia | 45.2 | 30.0 | 48.6 | 27.3 | 24.1 | 24.3 | 58.2 | 71.3 |
| Luxembourg | 54.2 | 59.6 | 40.3 | 37.1 | 23.8 | 31.0 | 23.3 | 41.5 |
| Morocco | 18.0 | 16.9 | 46.9 | 46.0 | 23.4 | 20.9 | 86.5 | 88.0 |
| Netherlands | 55.0 | 51.3 | 42.2 | 41.6 | 21.6 | 26.3 | 33.4 | 50.7 |
| Norway | 31.8 | 41.6 | 51.3 | 33.0 | 45.7 | 15.7 | 34.3 | 24.0 |
| Oman | 42.7 | 46.1 | 82.2 | 69.3 | 23.9 | 30.6 | 89.1 | 91.0 |

TABLE A9   (continued)

| | "To make a difference in the world" | "To build great wealth or very high income" | "To continue a family tradition" | "To earn a living because jobs are scarce" |
|---|---|---|---|---|
| Panama | 65.4 | 50.1 | 39.0 | 78.4 |
| Poland | 16.0 | 62.5 | 12.5 | 53.4 |
| Qatar | 46.5 | 77.3 | 37.4 | 54.8 |
| Republic of Korea | 9.0 | 71.1 | 4.1 | 34.3 |
| Romania | 65.9 | 64.9 | 31.1 | 75.0 |
| Russian Federation | 27.6 | 65.3 | 20.8 | 68.9 |
| Saudi Arabia | 63.7 | 78.6 | 65.5 | 82.8 |
| Slovak Republic | 18.7 | 22.1 | 25.8 | 89.8 |
| Slovenia | 61.8 | 42.6 | 27.4 | 63.8 |
| South Africa | 81.4 | 83.3 | 63.2 | 84.7 |
| Spain | 43.2 | 38.0 | 19.7 | 72.4 |
| Sudan | 49.3 | 86.8 | 56.8 | 87.7 |
| Sweden | 45.3 | 55.0 | 20.6 | 28.0 |
| Switzerland | 57.9 | 51.5 | 14.1 | 46.8 |
| Turkey | 34.3 | 39.9 | 41.7 | 55.0 |
| United Arab Emirates | 66.1 | 78.7 | 49.7 | 68.8 |
| United Kingdom | 53.0 | 55.2 | 21.7 | 63.8 |
| United States | 71.2 | 74.1 | 41.5 | 45.8 |
| Uruguay | 38.7 | 38.8 | 25.0 | 71.3 |

| | "To make a difference in the world" | | "To build great wealth or very high income" | | "To continue a family tradition" | | "To earn a living because jobs are scarce" | |
|---|---|---|---|---|---|---|---|---|
| | 18–34 | 35–64 | 18–34 | 35–64 | 18–34 | 35–64 | 18–34 | 35–64 |
| Panama | 65.8 | 65.0 | 54.5 | 46.4 | 40.7 | 37.6 | 80.4 | 76.8 |
| Poland | 14.1 | 18.0 | 46.8 | 77.8 | 8.9 | 16.1 | 36.7 | 70.0 |
| Qatar | 46.9 | 46.0 | 79.4 | 74.6 | 37.5 | 37.2 | 54.9 | 54.7 |
| Republic of Korea | 7.5 | 9.5 | 68.7 | 71.9 | 6.0 | 3.5 | 16.4 | 40.3 |
| Romania | 76.6 | 59.0 | 72.4 | 60.3 | 25.1 | 34.8 | 73.3 | 76.1 |
| Russian Federation | 26.1 | 28.8 | 67.8 | 63.3 | 15.3 | 25.1 | 70.4 | 67.7 |
| Saudi Arabia | 63.7 | 63.8 | 76.8 | 79.9 | 67.3 | 64.3 | 81.9 | 83.4 |
| Slovak Republic | 26.7 | 12.6 | 27.4 | 18.0 | 25.7 | 25.9 | 92.9 | 87.5 |
| Slovenia | 64.2 | 59.0 | 43.4 | 41.6 | 20.8 | 35.5 | 62.3 | 65.7 |
| South Africa | 83.2 | 78.5 | 84.4 | 81.4 | 64.4 | 61.3 | 87.5 | 80.0 |
| Spain | 52.4 | 39.6 | 49.5 | 33.5 | 21.8 | 18.9 | 68.2 | 74.0 |
| Sudan | 48.2 | 50.8 | 86.5 | 87.3 | 52.7 | 62.5 | 86.8 | 88.9 |
| Sweden | 53.9 | 39.9 | 70.1 | 45.4 | 27.1 | 16.5 | 37.0 | 22.4 |
| Switzerland | 56.9 | 58.4 | 65.9 | 45.3 | 12.4 | 14.8 | 41.3 | 49.1 |
| Turkey | 32.9 | 35.7 | 49.7 | 29.7 | 38.4 | 45.1 | 55.3 | 54.6 |
| United Arab Emirates | 67.0 | 65.0 | 81.5 | 75.2 | 48.5 | 51.2 | 73.1 | 63.6 |
| United Kingdom | 57.9 | 48.7 | 61.7 | 49.6 | 20.6 | 22.5 | 68.2 | 60.1 |
| United States | 73.5 | 69.5 | 78.7 | 70.6 | 49.4 | 35.5 | 48.2 | 44.0 |
| Uruguay | 35.8 | 41.2 | 47.5 | 31.0 | 20.9 | 28.6 | 74.0 | 68.8 |

TABLE A10    National Entrepreneurship Context Index and number of Entrepreneurial Framework Conditions (EFCs) scored as sufficient or better (score ≥5)

|  | Income level | Number of Entrepreneurial Framework Conditions (EFCs) scored as sufficient or better | NECI score |
|---|---|---|---|
| Belarus | Level B | 3 | 3.6 |
| Brazil | Level C | 2 | 3.6 |
| Canada | Level A | 6 | 5.1 |
| Chile | Level B | 5 | 4.5 |
| Colombia | Level C | 6 | 4.7 |
| Croatia | Level B | 2 | 3.9 |
| Cyprus | Level B | 3 | 4.2 |
| Dominican Republic | Level C | 3 | 3.7 |
| Egypt | Level C | 3 | 4.4 |
| Finland | Level A | 12 | 6.2 |
| France | Level A | 8 | 5.1 |
| Germany | Level A | 7 | 5.1 |
| Greece | Level B | 2 | 4.4 |
| Guatemala | Level C | 4 | 3.8 |
| Hungary | Level B | 3 | 4.5 |
| India | Level C | 5 | 5.0 |
| Iran | Level C | 2 | 3.3 |
| Ireland | Level A | 6 | 4.7 |
| Israel | Level A | 4 | 4.9 |
| Italy | Level A | 3 | 4.7 |
| Jamaica | Level C | 2 | 4.2 |
| Japan | Level A | 2 | 4.7 |
| Kazakhstan | Level B | 7 | 4.8 |
| Latvia | Level B | 6 | 5.0 |
| Lithuania | Level B | 12 | 6.1 |
| Luxembourg | Level A | 7 | 4.9 |
| Mexico | Level C | 4 | 4.3 |
| Morocco | Level C | 2 | 3.9 |
| Netherlands | Level A | 12 | 6.3 |

| | Income level | Number of Entrepreneurial Framework Conditions (EFCs) scored as sufficient or better | NECI score |
|---|---|---|---|
| Norway | Level A | 10 | 5.7 |
| Oman | Level B | 2 | 4.1 |
| Panama | Level B | 1 | 3.9 |
| Poland | Level B | 3 | 4.2 |
| Qatar | Level A | 11 | 5.5 |
| Republic of Korea | Level A | 8 | 5.7 |
| Romania | Level B | 2 | 4.0 |
| Russian Federation | Level B | 3 | 4.1 |
| Saudi Arabia | Level A | 12 | 6.1 |
| Slovak Republic | Level B | 2 | 4.3 |
| Slovenia | Level B | 4 | 4.3 |
| South Africa | Level C | 0 | 3.7 |
| Spain | Level B | 10 | 5.4 |
| Sudan | Level C | 1 | 3.2 |
| Sweden | Level A | 6 | 5.3 |
| Switzerland | Level A | 10 | 5.5 |
| Turkey | Level B | 2 | 4.2 |
| United Arab Emirates | Level A | 13 | 6.8 |
| United Kingdom | Level A | 6 | 4.9 |
| United States | Level A | 8 | 5.3 |
| Uruguay | Level B | 4 | 4.3 |

# Bibliography

ANI (3 September 2022), India pips UK to become 5th largest economy; here is what analysts say. The Print. (Retrieved from India pips UK to become 5th largest economy; here is what analysts say – ThePrint – ANIFeed on 6 October 2022).

About Indian Economy Growth Rate & Statistics. (April 2021). India Brand Equity Foundation. https://www.ibef.org/economy/indian-economy-ovrview

COVID-19 Innovation Development Accelerator. C-CAMP. https://www.ccamp.res.in/covid-19-innovations-deployment-accelerator

Department for Promotion of Industry and Internal Trade. Startup India. The Women Entrepreneurship Platform (WEP). Ministry of Commerce and Industry. https://www.startupindia.gov.in/content/sih/en/government-scheme/Wep.html

Department for Promotion of Industry and Internal Trade. (January 2021). Ease of Doing Business in India. Ministry of Commerce and Industry. Government of India.

Department for Promotion of Industry and Internal Trade. Start-up India. The Women Entrepreneurship Platform (WEP). Ministry of Commerce and Industry. https://www.startupindia.gov.in/content/sih/en/government-schemes/Wep.html

Economic Survey 2021-22, Ministry of Finance, Government of India.

Economic Survey 2020-21 (Volume-1). Ministry of Finance. Government of India

Economic Survey 2020-21 (Volume-2). Ministry of Finance. Government of India

Global Startup Ecosystem Index (2021). Startup Blink

Global Entrepreneurship Monitor. National Expert Survey. https://www.gemconsortium.org/wiki/1142

Global Entrepreneurship Monitor Global Report. https://www.gemconsortium.org/file/open?field=50691

Global Entrepreneurship Monitor. 2021/2022 Global Report. https://www.gemconsortium.org/reports/latest-global-report

Global Entrepreneurship Monitor. India Report 2020-21. https://www.gemindiaconsortium.org/gem_india_report.html

Handbook of Statistics on Indian Economy (2022), Reserve Bank of India.

Health Tech India Report (2021), Tracxn 2021.

Periodic Labour Force Survey, Various Years, EPW Research Foundation.

Spigel, Ben (2020). Entrepreneurial Ecosystems. Edward Elgar Publishing Limited (2020).

Shukla, s.Bharti, P. and Dwivedi, A.K. (2021). Global Entrepreneurship Monitor India Report 2019-20. https://www.gemindiaconsortium.org/gem_news-5.html

Shukla, S., Chatwal, S, Navniit, Bharti, P., Dwivedi, A.K. Shastri, V. (2020). Global Entrepreneurship Monitor India Report 2018-19. https://gemindiaconsortium.org/reports/GEM%20India%20Report%20 2018-19.pdf

Shukla,S., Parray, MI., Singh,C., Bharti, P. and Dwivedi, A.K. (2019) Global Entrepreneurship Monitor. India Report 2017-18. https://www.gemconsortium.org/report/global-entrepreneurship-monitor-india-report-2017-18

States' Start-up Ranking 2021, Department for Promotion of Industry and Internal Trade, Ministry of Commerce and Industry, Government of India.

T-HUB in Hyderabad. COVID-19 innovation challenge in partnership with Q-City. https://t-hub.co/covid-19-innovation-challenge/#

World Economic Outlook (2022), International Monetary Fund.

World Trade Report (2021), Economic Resilience and Trade, World Trade Organization.

World Competitiveness ranking. IMD. https://www.imd.org/centers/world-competitiveness-center/ rankings/world-competitiveness

For Product Safety Concerns and Information please contact our EU
representative  GPSR@taylorandfrancis.com
Taylor & Francis Verlag GmbH, Kaufingerstraße 24, 80331 München, Germany